Praise for *The Other World We Live In*

"Where are the angels these days? No doubt, they mind their own business. And a great business it is: that of God's ultimate plan for the created world. The real question is where are *we* in the cosmic battle that engages the opposing armies of Heaven and Hell? This beautiful and terrible book ('terrible' in the best sense, like Our Lady, who is said to be, *terrible as an army in battle array*) elucidates the part we are to play in the drama unfolding all around us on an invisible plane. How can we afford to miss out on this vision?"

— ABBOT PHILIP ANDERSON, Our Lady of Clear Creek Abbey

"In sparkling, spirited prose, Scott Paine addresses the modern world's appalling amnesia regarding the nature and history of the angelic orders, and their demonic counterparts. The result is a thoroughly engaging guidebook to the world of spirits, ranging from Our Lady's relationship with angels to the reasons why devils are falling as well as fallen, to the arsenal of demon-busting weapons in the Catholic armory. Throughout, Paine's scholarship, wit, and insight never flag, producing a book that will be happily read by the choirs of heaven as well as the faithful here on earth."

— PHILIP ZALESKI, Smith College

"The author integrates insights into the world of angels and demons with Christian spirituality, buttressing what we profess in the Nicene Creed, namely, our faith in one God, the maker of all things visible and invisible. Reflections regarding the nature and mission of these spirits, both good and evil, assist the reader in whetting the all-important tools of discernment between light and darkness. We are made acutely aware that our struggle is not against flesh and blood. We are spurred on to a more intimate, enlightened friendship with the good angels, reliving moments when mortals ate angelic bread. The whole is couched in theologically refined language and a style at the same time gripping, stirring, and uplifting."

— FR. ANDREAS HOECK, St. John Vianney Theological Seminary

"Yet another Catholic book on angels? Thus I mused as I began to read *The Other World We Live In*. But the first page changed all that. Paine has authored a masterpiece of angelology. Crisply concise, it nevertheless covers the topic comprehensively: cosmologically, metaphysically, psychologically, scripturally, spiritually. His treatment of the fall of the angels is the best I've read, and the latter part is a masterclass on spiritual warfare. Yes, I read Saint Thomas Aquinas's treatise (and several other works) on the angels, but not till I engaged this *tour de force* did I realize how essential are the angels in every aspect of life."

—THADDEUS KOZINSKI, Divine Mercy University

"There are truths beyond our comprehension, truths we may know to be true but never fully comprehend. In our myopic-scientistic culture, such truths — like those concerning the angels — are often labelled as fantasies. Drawing upon the intellectual traditions of far wiser cultures, Fr. Scott Randall Paine illuminates how the angels foster the coherence of the spiritual world with the visible world. That is, how the solidity, reality, and diversity of these 'separate substances' engage with each other and as well with human beings, the Church, the unfolding of history, Christ and His Blessed Mother, and sin. This remarkable book also provides practical bearings toward living with these hierarchical beings, as understood in the light of Christian faith."

—BRIAN KEMPLE, Lyceum Institute

"The angelic world so surpasses our limited understanding that we need to approach it with both theological precision and poetic insight. In *The Other World We Live In*, Fr. Paine deftly leads us on such an exploration, emphasizing the light and glory of the holy angels, but also giving due attention to the dark world of demons. His presentation is balanced and at times humorous, leading one to understand why Chesterton said 'angels can fly because they can take themselves lightly.'"

—FR. GARY SELIN, St. John Vianney Theological Seminary

The Other World We Live In

The Other World We Live In

A Catholic Vision
of Angelic Reality

SCOTT RANDALL PAINE

Angelico Press

We have now received a truth which must be profoundly important for every Christian: that there are pure spirits, creatures of God, initially all good and then, through a choice of sin, irreducibly separated into angels of light and angels of darkness. —POPE ST. JOHN PAUL II

CONTENTS

PROLOGUE
So Much We Don't See

BEFORE APPROACHING THE TOPIC OF angels, we should be reminded that a consideration of invisible realities need hardly be arcane, or the subject matter as "supernatural" as one might suspect. Reflect, for a moment, on a few dimensions of the world we take to be quite real, but cannot pick up with our senses:

1) Spatially: There is far more world, more cosmos, out there than your eyes can even approximately capture — immeasurably more. This is true whether we limit ourselves to the expanse of the earth or include the one trillion galaxies currently spotted in our universe. That vast context, though unseen, both contains and conditions what you do see and experience. And these veiled immensities you accept without ever viewing them, and you are right in doing so.

2) Chronologically: There are always thousands of years of past time — and if we think geologically, millions — which you never can experience, or even remember, and yet which have profoundly influenced your world, and all that is in it. And even more out of view lies the unpredictable future. All this you also accept as real (or soon to be so), although it is not part of your sensory experience.

3) Scientifically: We accept as a matter of fact that there are quadrillions of atoms buzzing within us and around us, but we cannot see a single one of them. Even light we actually never see in its own right; we see things *in* light, but the light itself (along with all other forms of electromagnetic radiation) never slips as such into our field of vision. We also promptly answer our cell phones, firmly convinced of the existence of highways of invisible radiation passing between them and our interlocutors.

But nothing drives this home more dramatically than the following: for decades astrophysicists have been cautioning us that the vaunted conquests of modern science have only shown us about

5% of all the material reality that exists. The other 95% — so-called "dark matter and energy" — still remains largely unidentified. Nonetheless, this invisible world has an enormous impact on the modest 5% that we do (more or less) understand.

Thus, on a material basis alone, any scientifically enlightened view of reality must concede that beyond the tiny slice of cosmos we are able to perceive, there is incalculably more that is unseen. And despite its invisibility — whether intrinsic or due to circumstance — we tranquilly and confidently affirm its existence.

Now add to all this a fourth, and even more emphatically undisputed, fact:

4) Virtually all known historical cultures and religions have accepted the existence of one sort or another of subtle material or completely immaterial beings, usually of a personal nature. Among countless others, we read of hierarchies of Greco-Roman, Egyptian, Mesopotamian, Celtic, Nordic, Indian, Chinese, Andean or Meso-American gods, along with sprites, genies, fairies, elemental spirits, *kamis* and an almost limitless variety of minor deities. Only a small number of traditional skeptics of the past and (of course) today's confessional materialists have ever disputed this.

The irony is that contemporary naysayers inevitably call on modern science to underwrite their twilight of the gods. But despite their appeals, recent physics is often more skeptical about the solidity of the matter these doubters place their faith in, than about the reality of the spirits whose existence they impugn. And even more telling is this: science and faith, contrary to expectations, have joined hands in one incontrovertible claim — they agree that the totality of all that exists contains *far more* than what we can see and touch with our senses, explain with our reason, or even detect with our most sophisticated instruments. Far from coddling us in our doubts about spirits, today's science gives us little warrant, and even less excuse, for excluding the angels from our conspectus of reality.

PART 1
Angels On High

"The Celestial Rose" by Gustave Doré

INTRODUCTION
"Separate Substances" Today

A FEW YEARS AGO, THE BRITISH COME-
dian Stephen Fry spoke on television about a recently
completed tour through the United States. He had many
good things to say about the Yankees, and although a convinced
atheist, still showed respect for the robust Christianity of so many
Americans. Nonetheless, he could not help remarking with alarm
on one item of faith that he found particularly bizarre: many of
them still believe in angels!

Since wide-spread misunderstanding prevails in any use of the
word "angel," I choose to introduce my reflections by using the
medieval, metaphysical term for the pure spirits. We might preempt
Mr. Fry's outrage by reminding him that what we are really talking
about are beings with intellectual and volitional endowments, and
that exist separately from matter: in philosophical jargon, "separate
substances." This will hardly convert him, but it may convince him
that what he does *not* know about angels could — just possibly — be
far greater than what is conveyed by the frivolous caricatures he,
and the rest of us, are familiar with.

Indeed, today we are in a bad way when we try to think intel-
ligently about angels. Even those who still believe in them are not
much better off. More often than not, they will think of spirits as
wispy and rarefied, passing through our world like a morning fog.
Here they come, smiling and fluttering, like ethereal butterflies,
casting pixie dust over our benighted world. We might expect
help from sacred art, but here too we are frequently misled. How
often do we see Renaissance and Baroque depictions of cute,
bare-bottomed "cherubim" (embarrassingly called *putti* in artistic
lingo)? Even worse, we might also see God's spirits presented as
wan, effeminate figures resembling kindly Caucasian ladies in flowing evening gowns.

Sometimes the only antidote to these silly fantasies is to encounter one of our world's pre-literate tribal cultures; they still know

that spirits are not to be messed with. Or perhaps we could listen to an interview with a good, experienced exorcist. These gentlemen know only too well that we are speaking of powerful realities, albeit, in this case, from the darker side.

My intention here is to convey the reality of a world we also live in, but one that our senses rarely perceive, and that our celebrated scientific outlook can often not even imagine. But it is a world that is real like mountains and stars are real. In fact, it is even more solid than the proud stone of the Rocky Mountains, and more radiant than the shining stars in the firmament. Spiritual reality is as real as it gets.

This does not mean, of course, that the material cosmos is unreal—far from it. Nonetheless, the Gnostic temptation of demoting material reality always lies in wait when we emphasize spiritual matters. But God positively willed the creation of matter; he destined all its mass and energy, along with the angels and our troubled human race, to a shared future of glory. Our problem is trying to keep all three components of creation in mind. We tend to waver between two false absolutes: a purely spiritual world (certain versions of Platonism and most versions of Gnosticism) or a purely material one (the naturalism so favored today).

In earlier times, when people opened their eyes upon the world of nature and the stars above us, their gaze reached far beyond our own. They saw how the spiritual and material worlds interpenetrate, cooperating in a revelation in which our own composite nature becomes, in the words of Thomas Aquinas, the *mirabilis connexio* (the amazing link). Far from being the summit of creation, we understood ourselves to be the meeting place and confluence of matter and spirit.

Our forebears not only detected the hand of a Creator God who made all these material wonders, but also the unmistakable signs of a world of pure created spirits, powerfully present within the concrete mysteries of nature. The angels seemed to wink at them as they mediated between the Almighty and those of us in the corporeal world. Our fellow humans of yesteryear would have regarded the arrogant eyes of the secular know-it-alls of today as blind, seeing only two dimensions, when there are three (or even more). They would have held our quantified scientific interpretation of nature to be not only partial, but even partisan. The scientist poring over these measurements would have seemed to them like someone able to see and scrutinize a musical score, but unable to hear the music.

Most of our languages, modern and classic, refer to spirits using words that originally meant air, wind or breath. Air is invisible, and yet it gives life; air is seemingly weak, and yet hurricanes and tornados are among the most violent of nature's outbursts. The fact is that spirits are not just ideas or values floating in some imagined stratosphere. Spirit is the most ontologically dense and operationally intense of all the varieties of being.

Moreover, spirits are not, strictly speaking, things at all, but rather "someones." In a word, they are persons. And persons are what the "spiritual" is all about. To put a fine point on it, a spirit is simply an immaterial being endowed with the two interior faculties of self-transcendence: intelligence and volition. Since we also possess these faculties, we too are spiritual, although linked amazingly to matter.

In the Abrahamic traditions, personhood is believed to exist in three irreducible forms: divine, angelic and human. Furthermore, personal reality is, again according to Thomas Aquinas, "the most perfect of all that exists in nature" (*perfectissimum in tota natura*). We instinctively know this, for when we insist on the "dignity of the human person," we are simply acknowledging this perfection in the only persons we have direct, palpable contact with: ourselves. But it applies at least equally to the angels, and of course immeasurably more to God.

In saner times the existence of personal, spiritual beings would have been among the commonsense coordinates of all intelligent earthlings. The doubters would have been the oddballs. In fact, in those days, after a long conversation with Mr. Fry, someone may well have walked away and commented on how polite and witty the comedian was, but then lowered their voice and whispered, as if revealing a dark secret: "... but the poor man does not even believe in angels!"

I
God's Three-Fold Creation

C HRISTIANS HOLD THAT THERE ARE three *hypostases*, or "Persons" in the Godhead: Father, Son and Holy Spirit. As creatures, we discover there are also three distinct worlds in creation: the world of matter and energy (the cosmos, including the lower life forms), the world of humanity, and the world of the pure spirits, whom we call angels. This is a virtually universal tradition, and corresponds, it would seem, to a very fundamental human experience of the hierarchy of reality. Old Testament revelation has confirmed this experience and added its own voice to the traditions of the world. We find this first intimated in the opening words of the book of Genesis: "In the beginning, God created the heavens and the earth."

Although the "heavens" first address our visual imagination with the spectacle of the vaulted sky, they further suggest everything that is *above* us. We will later see that the understanding of our place in the universe will always involve an "up" and "down," at the very least symbolically (see ch. 4, *Excursus* 2). Our physical sky stands as a kind of sovereign symbol for the spiritual world on high, and of all those who live and act "up there." Heaven and "the heavens," as terms of reference, are difficult to separate in the anglophone imagination; some languages even lack a separate word for "sky." They use the same word to speak of both the physical sky, or "the heavens," and the spiritual heaven (in German, for instance: *der Himmel*; or in Portuguese: *o céu*). For the Christian, in the words of the *Catechism* of 1992, heaven is simply "the 'place' of the spiritual creatures, the angels, who surround God" (CCC n. 326).

The earth "down here," on the other hand, and according to the same compact Hebrew imagery, stands for the whole of physical creation in its complementary, if subordinate, relationship to the world of spirit. From the beginning, the angels were understood to exercise stewardship over the cosmos. However, a more intimate

9

contact between the realm of spirit and the realm of matter had to await the advent of the third creature in this unfolding scenario: man.

On the sixth day, after creating and forming all the vast hierarchies of angelic and material reality, God changed his language and spoke for the first time in the first person (or better, in first Persons): "Let us make man in our image, after our likeness." By exquisitely poising humanity midway between pure spirit and pure matter, the Triune God joined in a mysterious bond these three categories of created being: the angelic, the cosmic and the human.

As might be expected, each of the three divisions of creation brings to mind one of the three Divine Persons. The material cosmos, that "moving image of eternity" (to quote Plato) — from colossal galaxies down to subatomic particles — and from which biological life, in all its variety and beauty, will eventually emerge, reminds us of the Father, the Giver of Life. The human world, characterized by language and discourse, articulation and emphasis, points us instead to the *Logos*, the Son. It is he, after all, who will eventually take on a human nature. Finally, the realm of the created spirits — as mysterious and invisible in their virtual presence as they are powerful — invites us to ponder the *uncre-ated Holy* Spirit. It seems God willed to be mirrored in a most intimate way by his tripartite creation. At the end of Scripture, these three divisions are unmistakably present again, each participating fully in the final consummation of creation. We find this in the Apocalypse.

In chapter 21, as St. John looks upon the Heavenly Jerusalem, he sees the city has twelve gates. Through these gates, creation will gain entrance to its final fulfillment. Each has three principal constituents: jasper and other gems adorn the walls and the foundation stones, representing material creation; the inscribed names of the Twelve Apostles and of the Patriarchs of the Twelve Tribes of Israel representing human creation; and then, there is an angel at each gate. All of this suggests a most deep-rooted kinship and predestined cooperation between angel, man and cosmos.

A further trinitarian reflection might also be highlighted. The sheer vastness of the cosmos — measuring light-years of incalculable magnitude — suggests the grandeur and majesty of God the

Father, who is without beginning and without end. Cosmic order and intelligibility, in contrast, evoke the presence of the *Logos*, the Word that is the Second Person of the Holy Trinity. Here is the home of all those fabled Ideas, or Platonic Forms, impressing a luminous stamp of intelligible unity upon the world's multiplicity. And looking at it all from the perspective of cosmic time, the dynamism and evolution of the cosmos — dimensions of our universe that have come to our attention in modern astrophysics and cosmogony — evoke the movement of the Holy Spirit, both through human history and through eons of cosmogenesis. Even material reality is on a kind of pilgrimage, for it too is destined to partake of its due measure of God's glory in the New Jerusalem.[1]

This threefold handiwork of God belongs to the Church's spontaneous fund of theological references. In 1215, the 4th Council of the Lateran taught that "God by his almighty power created together in the beginning of time *both* creatures, the *spiritual* and the *corporeal*, namely the angelic and the earthly, and afterwards the *human*, as it were an intermediate creature, composed of body and spirit" (Denzinger, *Enchiridion Symbolorum et Definitionum*, 800 [428], my translation, emphasis added). In Pope St. John Paul's 1986 catechesis on the angels, he spoke of how we "admire, struck dumb with wonder, the great mystery of the intelligence and love of God, in his action of creation, directed to the *cosmos*, to the *human person*, and to the world of *pure spirits*" ("Catechesis on the Angels," 1986, part 6, no. 5, emphasis added).

The angels, therefore, are far more than an ornamental supplement to creation, or a mere "roof" of twinkling luminaries. They are the very first creatures of God, and just as integral to the whole of creation as are human beings and the orders of material reality, both inorganic and living. Ignoring the separate substances ought to be as serious an oversight as ignoring the bottom third of creation, the material world upon which we lavish so much love and attention. We have grown dull, though, through sin and age, and will need more than our five senses to keep this truth alive to our minds. As in so many other matters, the Faith comes to our rescue.

1 I owe this last Trinitarian reference to: Benedict Ashley and John Deely, *How Science Enriches Theology* (South Bend, IN: St. Augustine's Press, 2012).

One of the more recent credal statements of our Christian confession, issued by Pope St. Paul VI in June 1968, stands as a further magisterial assurance that the angels are here to stay. Unintimidated by contemporary secularism or materialist pundits, the pope proclaims our serene conviction in the existence of "things invisible such as the pure spirits, which are also called angels" (*Creed of the People of God*, n. 8).

A quarter of a century later the Church will be even more unambiguous: "The existence of the spiritual, non-corporeal beings that Sacred Scripture usually calls 'angels' is a truth of faith. The witness of Scripture is as clear as the unanimity of Tradition" (*Catechism*, 1992, n. 328). Our minds and hearts rejoice when reassured that there is more to reality than just molecules and atoms. Minds and hearts have always suspected as much.

2

Two Camps of Battle

"AND THERE WAS WAR IN HEAVEN" (APOC. 12:7). The simple statement embodied in those few words suggests an event of such magnitude, and couched in such an unaccustomed context, that we need to read it twice to absorb its full impact. Of war we have some experience, at least indirectly. But our ideas of heaven, even when aided by what was said in the last chapter, are at best rudimentary. At the very least, we imagine it to be a place of perpetual peace. Understandably, our imagination is cast into confusion by the attempt to wed our picture of paradise with any suggestion of warfare. But, again, Scripture assures us, "there was war in heaven."

What kind of battle can there be in the *spiritual* world? If "heaven" is still taken to signify the world of pure spirits, the war must have been, in some way, a contest among angels. Holy Scripture, and the consistent teaching of the Church, do bear witness to the existence of two camps of angels, the good and the bad. It was for this reason that the present book is divided into two parts. But how could such an apparently counterintuitive split occur in the world of God's most sublime creatures?

Explanations do not come easy in these matters. Perhaps the following reflections will help us to gain an appreciation of the issues at stake. We should begin by highlighting two fundamental mistakes we make when thinking about spiritual reality. One we have already mentioned before: the tendency to imagine spirits as wispy and homogeneous. Let us make the relevant correction even more emphatic by insisting that there is more firmness, even *solidity*, in the being of the pure spirits than what we witness here on earth in our stones and continents.

And what is more, there is even greater variety among them than what we admire in our thousands of plant and animal species. Spiritual reality is profoundly and manifoldly real, with more diversity and multiplicity than can be found in the world of cells, atoms and molecules. Here the Church has always chimed in with Plato about the robust reality, and indeed ontological diversity, of the transcendent orders of reality.

Nonetheless, there is another and more insidious confusion to be averted. It arises when we equate spirit — full stop — with goodness, and imagine that the more spiritual something is, the holier it must also be. This typically results in identifying matter, and especially our flesh, and "the thousand natural shocks that flesh is heir to," as the matrix of all that is evil. Most forms of Gnosticism, and especially Manichaeism, succumb to this beguilement.

We should know better, for even in human ethics, few will doubt that pride and hatred — sins of the spiritual will — are far more heinous than gluttony or lust. And even these more carnal urges become truly sinful only when the spiritual will consents to their disorders. So, the point must be made with every possible emphasis: spiritual reality is not only ontologically, but *also morally* heterogeneous. The varieties of angels are incomparably more sundry than are the endless shelves of products in our biggest megastores, and the moral gulf between good and bad spirits out-yawns even the chasm between a Hitler and a St. Thérèse of Lisieux.

Of course, evil is infamously parasitical. And in matters of knowledge, every error hinges, inevitably, upon one or another misunderstood truth. Furthermore, we are not *entirely* off base when we tend to associate mortal sin with carnal sin. It is a proven fact that spiritual transgression weakens us in the face of more "down-to-earth," carnal temptations. And carnal sin is, as we know, quite limited in its resources. Moreover, though sin in the spiritual world is varied, it can never match, or even get close to, the prolific fecundity of goodness.

The many-splendored array of virtue's achievements infinitely outshines the grey boredom of sin's limited assortments. Pornography's inevitable "ho-hum" repetitiveness is proof of this. Sin, when all is said and done, has very few tricks in its bag. Look, in contrast, at the inexhaustible array of *kinds* of sanctity, *varieties* of holiness and *medleys* of virtue on display in the Church's saints. Although spirit is certainly higher than matter, matter was made to reflect that sublimity and participate in it. God has made the world of matter to shine supernaturally with his spiritual gifts. One need look no further than at the face of a happy infant, or at the spread of stars overhead at night, or at the ocean from any earthly shore. These spectacles are immediately stunning and eloquent with a wordless language. It is in dark minds and perverted wills that we must look for the sources of evil, and not in a material reality the very destiny of which is to reflect all that is beautiful and sublime.

Nonetheless, we hold on stubbornly to our images of spirituality as all sweetness and light. We still find the notion of a heavenly battlefield an oxymoron, to say the least. There is a way, however, to make the matter more approachable. This is something that ought to be quite familiar: namely, our very own wars of words and ideas.

In the heavens we carry in our heads — that is, in the world of notions and thoughts within our own skulls — everything from minor conceptual skirmishes to major ideological altercations are frequently on display. The most war-torn combat zone on earth extends between our two ears. The famous 16th-century spiritual writer Lorenzo Scupoli had no need to think twice before entitling his manual on the interior life of the Christian. He called it *The Spiritual Combat*.

There is no dearth of examples of this immaterial battlefield in recent history. Let us consider just one. We are forever reminded of the misdeeds of the 20th century's favorite villain, Adolf Hitler. But his revolting external acts were thrown up out of the perverted ponderings from deep within the same man's mind. It was back when he sat peacefully in prison, in Germany's Landsberg am Lech, in the mid-1920s. Thinking hard and with iron will, he went to war intellectually with all that is good and true. Quietly, and logically, he dictated his book, *Mein Kampf*. Ideas have consequences.

We can develop this even further. Virtually all of our human wars find their ultimate causes in the world of ideas, that is, in the "heavens" of our own minds. That such could be the case with the pure spirits ought not to surprise us. "Intelligences," by the way, is another philosophical name for the angels. However, this can mislead us into forgetting that spiritual beings also have wills. Intelligence in God's creatures always stands in tandem with the powers of intellectual appetition, which we call volition. Intellects and wills are inseparable in creatures endowed with spirit, whether angel or man; the same is true of their operations.

Before the intellect can enjoy the coveted light of genuine insight, the will must generate the volitional energy of desiring to know. Fire is only true fire if it produces both light *and* warmth.

Genuine and proportioned truth for the intellect only comes when accompanied by corresponding goodness in the will. Knowledge and love are just as intimately wed in spiritual reality as are light and warmth in the material world. They were designed to grow together, but often enough find themselves at odds. A telltale red flag of intellectual mischief appears when we learn that truth and goodness have been interrogated in separate rooms. Isolating them by design inevitably figures in all infernal recipes of temptation.

Theological tradition teaches us that after God created the angels, he submitted them to a test. The first human beings, we know from Genesis, also had to endure a trial. But before writing off these narratives as Bronze Age mythology, we might be surprised to discover that the story is far more familiar to our everyday lives than we might think.

It belongs to the very nature of the learning experience that we be challenged in the will in order to be enlightened in the mind. Only if you are *willing* to trust your teacher will you be able to be taught. Only by *willing* to endure the hardship of long practice can you ever learn to play an instrument. Our wills came into the bargain once God resolved to invite us to true beatitude. The most astounding, and most confounding, of all God's creations is the miracle of freedom. Spiritual creatures (both disincarnate and incarnate) were granted this precarious endowment out of God's deepest divine love.

Since God built into human and angelic nature the ability to enjoy, *to the full*, his spiritual life, light and love, those creatures had to be able to choose and thus have the incomparable bliss of knowing they have chosen well. After all, God created the world in his own freedom. It makes sense that his infinite love would invite us to share in this freedom and, in some participated way, to make it our own. *This* is key for understanding the role of our trials.

Still, just how was this test possible for a pure spirit? In the 13th century, Thomas Aquinas struggled with the question in his last writings. Before his premature death, he was only able to conclude that in order to sin, the angel would have to somehow "turn away" from a good proposed by God. In the next generation, the Franciscan theologian Duns Scotus explored this further, and in the early 17th century, the Jesuit Francisco Suárez developed even more what Scotus had suggested. Good things can be expected when a Dominican, a Franciscan and a Jesuit put their minds together.

Suárez proposed that God revealed to the angels his plan for the creation of man, and that he intended to become human and be adored in that lowly form, even by the angels. The angels would have grasped enough of God's agenda to perceive that it was beyond their usual calculations and could only be accepted in humility and intellectual submission. Here we have all the ingredients for a trial.

This understanding of the angels' trial does give us an insight into the mystery of freedom. According to this premise, all the angels would have been impacted by the provocation of this mysterious design. As with the trial of our first parents, the creature would be asked to submit to a condition it did not fully comprehend. Seemingly a dodge, but actually a discipline — as when parents justify their commands with the words "because I said so" — this tempering of the will is actually a priming of the person (in both intellect *and* will) for an imminent lesson. It is aptly evoked by the image of the forbidden fruit of tempting knowledge, along with the sad spectacle of Eden slowly receding. However, what may be a Shakespearean drama for us is for the angels an instantaneous decision.

This truth is reflected even in our most beloved fairy tales. A typically unexplained stipulation is laid down as the condition for the attainment of final happiness (Don't pick that flower! Be back by midnight sharp!). Furthermore, the fun of sports depends in no small way on a number of rather arbitrary rules, the breaking of which means you lose, or at least get put on the bench. We observe this even when children invent their own games. We smile as we hear them mandating, "Let's say you have to...," whereby a whimsical regulation is decreed. The kids tacitly assume that only by blindly observing a rather capricious commandment will the participants have the freedom to play and be able to enjoy the fun of the sport.

Whatever the provocation of the trial, the rest belongs to our common theological tradition. After this trying moment, a chorus of holy affirmation rang out through the angelic ranks. God exclaimed with a divine command: "Let there be light!" — and indescribable beams of luminosity raced through the minds of all who had assented to God's unfathomable plan. The will's humility and submission promptly unlocked the mind's access to the bliss of understanding.

Aristotle taught that we all, by nature, desire to know. How right he was, but how little could he have suspected all this might imply. Even the angels longed to know about God, but only the gift of their wills and the proof of their love could unlock the lessons. Those lessons were not only beyond human logic but also answered questions that had not even been formulated.

The spirits that had till then been cautiously poised in merely created considerations were suddenly ecstatic. Since angels are

persons — and thus involved in personal relations among themselves — it should not strike us as unusual that their narrative
includes protagonists and a cast of characters. The Apocalypse
teaches that one humble angel had led the way to this light (Apoc.
12:7–9). Although he had been shaken, together with all the angels,
by the inscrutable strategies of God, his signal humility had made
him strong. He is also mentioned in the Book of Daniel (Dan. 10,
12), and also in the Epistle of Jude. Offhand references in the
written tradition of the Bible bear witness to a more completely
articulated version of the same in oral tradition. The very ease of
these references to St. Michael, as also the myriads of his depictions in sacred art, betray a profound Christian familiarity with
the story of this towering supernatural hero.

When confronted with the demonic bid to emulate divinity, and with not even a pose of pretended valiance, he simply
asked — almost like a schoolboy — the inevitable question, "*Who is
like unto God?*" This was a rhetorical question if ever there was
one. That humble query was destined to become his very name,
Michael: in Hebrew, *mi* (who) *ka-el* (is like God?). Led by this
self-effacing Archangel, all the choirs of angels sang (and have
sung ever since): *Holy, Holy, Holy, Lord God of Hosts! Heaven and
earth are full of your glory...*

"*And there was light, and God saw that the light was good.*"

When the vault of our earthly sky is replete with light, no
one thinks of the black, abysmal "outer space" just miles beyond.
And why should we? Black is an absence of light, and cannot and
should not be pondered, any more than one should step on holes
or read blanks. Shining a flashlight on the darkness in order to
understand it will not reveal anything except your own stupidity.
And so, at the first "Let there be light!" of creation, hardly a mind
took notice that an entire corps of created spirits had sunk back
into its own preferred version of reality. They countered God's
mysterious invitation to rejoice in the adventures of "Yes!" with
their own emphatic mantra of control: "No!"

"*And God separated the light from the darkness...*"

The holy angels found themselves sundered off from a throng of fellow creatures who had chosen to reject everything they could not understand, and thus could not control. Instead, they tried to "create" their own world, a counter-universe ruled by their own whim and illuminated only by their own neon-like glimmer. The Apocalypse (Apoc. 12:4) teaches that "his [the dragon's] tail swept down a third of the stars of heaven." It has been surmised, not without some relief, that this text suggests that only about a third of all angels fell (Part 2, chap. 3 of the present book).

God then imposed the separation of the good and bad angels. The obedient angels became "light," and God saw that it was good — the others became darkness, and God no longer looked upon them. In this first account of creation, little more is said about them — so unworthy of comment, and so inflated when referred to. But one last mention is made, and this regarding their work:

"*God called the light day, and the darkness he called night.*"

The one camp shared in the light of goodness, and works for the light — to extend, steward and protect it. The other camp shares in the black darkness, and the sardonic gloom of the "Light-Bearer" (Lucifer). His light was eclipsed by the cloud of his pride. He now works with his accomplices to extend, steward and protect the darkness. Still, he often masquerades as a kind of light, for "even Satan disguises himself as an angel of light" (2 Cor. 11:14). The night will always have its moments in history, or at most its hour. "This is your hour and the power of darkness," Our Lord said to Judas (Lk. 22:53). But afterwards will always follow the light:

"*And there was evening and there was morning, one day*" (Gn. 1:5).

It is significant that the Hebrew speaks here of the "one" day, and not the "first" day — cardinal and not ordinal like the remaining days. Scripture seems to be saying that this one day is the grand context — both ontological and moral — within which the other days will unfold as in a spiral, and our long, meandering story within this tension, will slowly be told.

Evening has its hour—morning has its day. As Pope St. Paul VI emphasized: "The evil which exists in the world is the result and effect of an attack upon us and our society by a dark and hostile agent, the Devil.... We know that this dark and destructive being really exists and is still active.... It would be very important to return to a study of Catholic teaching on the Devil and the influence he is able to wield, but nowadays little attention is paid to it" (Address, Nov. 15, 1972).

Both Vatican II and John Paul II, and more recently Pope Francis, have lent their voices to the Church's appeal that we not forget how we stand, not only between heaven and earth in the order of being but also between angel and demon in the order of moral choice. The angels have already chosen their sides in the battle for or against God. From now on, our choices are the only ones that matter. In the second part of our book, we will take a closer look at these spiritual prodigals. For now, we must direct our gazes toward him from whom they diverted theirs. We must learn to keep our attention focused on the one and only Lord.

3

The One Lord

T HE VOCATION OF JACOB, FATHER OF THE
Twelve Tribes of Israel, was given when he was shown a ladder
extending from heaven to earth; upon this ladder, the angels
of God were ascending and descending (Gn. 28). The patriarch of the
Chosen People beheld the Lord God standing above this heaven's
ladder, uttering for the first time the grand promise regarding his
descendants. The patriarch was profoundly shaken and exclaimed:
"How awesome is this place! This is none other than the house of
God, and this is the gate of heaven" (Gn. 28:17). Heaven and earth
connected by a ladder; angels ascending and descending; the house
of God and the gate of heaven; and the one Lord standing over it all.

That angel-studded occasion signaled the birth of the Israelites.
A corresponding scene in the New Testament marks the parallel
beginning of the public life of Christ, and of the founding of the
New Israel.

At the end of the first chapter of St. John's Gospel, our Lord promises a somewhat flustered Nathanael: "You will see heaven opened,
and the angels of God ascending and descending upon the Son of
Man" (Jn. 1:51). The ladder, seen prophetically by Jacob, is none
other than Christ himself. God the Father stands over his threefold
creation; but in Christ, all three parts are harmonized and brought
to their final perfection. By way of the Son of Man, the freeway of
angelic commerce between heaven and earth shall be reopened to
its holy traffic. Thus unfolds, as St. Paul teaches, the "plan for the
fullness of time, to unite *all things* in Him, things in heaven [the
angels], and things on earth [man and the cosmos]" (Eph. 1:10).

St. Thomas Aquinas teaches that Christ is Head not only of all
men, but also of all the angels (*Summa Theologiae*, III, 8.4). If it be
true that the Incarnation of the Word was the subject of the trial of
the angels at the beginning, then those first creatures of God have
been ordered in a special way to Christ from the very outset. This
was Duns Scotus's contention, and Scripture seems to agree: "In him
all things were created, in heaven and on earth, visible and invisible,
whether Thrones or Dominations or Principalities or Virtues — all
things were created through him and for him" (Col. 1:15–16).

Also, after we bring the spiritual battle into the picture, we find
that the final resolution of the conflict of sin also involves an ordering
of angel and material cosmos to Christ. St. Paul continues: "For in
him all the fullness of God was pleased to dwell, and through him to

reconcile to himself all things, whether *on earth or in heaven*, making peace by the Blood of his Cross" (Col. 1:20). What began as the obscure mystery of their trial becomes now the object of their deepest yearning. And it is not just the glorified God-Man that they yearn to understand, but also the darker mysteries of his Passion and Death. St. Peter writes in his first epistle of the "sufferings of Christ and the subsequent glory" as "things into which angels long to look" (1 Pt 1:12).

"Are they not all ministering servants sent forth to serve, for the sake of those who are to obtain salvation?" asks the Epistle to the Hebrews (Hb. 1:14). It seems, therefore, that the world of pure spirits situated above our human and material worlds has been ordered by God from the very beginning towards the mystery of Christ, and that the angels consequently have a most integral part to play in the drama of our salvation.

As St. John Paul II has taught, "In the key moments," the angels "surround Christ and accompany him in the fulfillment of his salvific mission in regard to mankind. In the same way also the whole of Tradition and the ordinary Magisterium of the Church down the centuries has attributed to the angels this particular character and this function of Messianic ministry" (Catechesis on the Angels, 1986, part 3, n. 4). They are far from being mere spectators.

Their appearance is always, as the Holy Father asserts, "in the key moments." What could be a more key moment than that of the Annunciation? (Lk. 1:26f.)

And who helped poor St. Joseph over his trial regarding the unexpected pregnancy of the Blessed Virgin? (Mt. 1:20f.)

Who were the first to proclaim and sing the praises of the newborn Christ? (Lk. 2:9f.)

And who guided the Holy Family to Egypt and back? (Mt. 2:13f.)

The angels were not merely indulging the Infant Jesus. As Christ begins his public ministry, and submits to the terrible temptation in the desert, Satan finally leaves him (that is, until the Passion), "and the angels ministered to him" (Mk. 1:13).

The reality of the angels, both holy and fallen, was frequently upon the lips of our Savior. In addition to the quote given above regarding the heaven's ladder, he refers to the "little ones," whose "angels always behold the face of my Father who is in heaven" (Mt. 18:10).

He comments before his Passion, that if he so desired, he could appeal to his Father, "and he will at once send me more than twelve legions of angels" (Mt. 26:53). He furthermore remarks that the blessed will not marry, but rather "are like angels in heaven" (Mk. 12:25), and that "he who denies me before men will be denied before the angels of God" (Lk. 12:9). And all penitents receive the specific assurance that "there is joy before the angels of God over one sinner who repents" (Lk. 15:10).

But nowhere in Our Lord's life do the angels step into such reverent proximity to his Person as in the Paschal Mystery itself. It is a revealed truth of enormous consequence, and still inviting deeper theological penetration, that while Our Lord's chosen Apostles were fast asleep, and his purest soul was flooded with the full horror of human sin, he was strengthened to endure his Passion for our salvation not by the Chosen People, not by his closest human friends, not even by his Mother, but by an angel (Lk. 22:43).

Christ's actual entrance into the Passion was, of course, an act he performed alone. All three divisions of creation witnessed in wonder that highest act of Christ which was his Passion. As would be his followers thereafter, so he too began as "a spectacle to the world, to angels and to men" (1 Cor. 4:9). But as it was only given to an angel to behold that last shiver on the face of Jesus as he fully laid his human will into the mystery of the divine, pressing the last bead of bloody sweat from his trembling Body, so it was only given to an angel to behold his triumphant exodus from the Passion: the Resurrection.

But this is not all. The fallen angels are also very much in the picture. Our Lord is constantly confronting the evil spirits, commanding them and banishing them from his path. Indeed, he understands his very Passion to be but one enormous exorcism: "Now is the judgment of this world, now shall the ruler of this world be cast out" (Jn. 12:32). The rebellious spirits had already recognized his extraordinary power and, in a way, were the first to proclaim his Messiahship. When one reads briskly through the Gospel of St. Mark, one cannot escape the impression that Jesus is a warrior. We look on as he strides decisively through a landscape dotted with enemy outposts, casting out demons to the right and to the left, and leaving a trail of human astonishment in his wake. After all, "The reason the Son of God appeared was to destroy the works of the devil" (1 Jn. 3:8).

Now the consummation of that grand exorcism is still forthcoming. Christ has performed it perfectly in his own human nature and in that of his Mother, but the fruits of that act have yet to be secured in the whole of his Mystical Body, the Church. *Our*

Paschal Mystery is still in progress.

It is when Christ refers to that final consummation that he begins to speak in a new way, and with a new insistence, about the reality and the role of the holy angels: "For the Son of Man is to come *with his angels* in the glory of his Father, and then he will repay every man for what he has done" (Mt. 16:26; Mk. 8:38). "He will send out the angels, and gather his elect from the four winds, from the ends *of the earth* to the ends *of heaven*" (Mk. 13:27; Mt. 13:41).

As we shall see later, the two angels who stay back with the Apostles as Christ leaves the earth and ascends into heaven (Acts 1:10) are themselves a reminder that the spirits of God will have an active and important role to play in the newly established Church. That role will increase and deepen as the Church's history unfolds. Finally, as the mysteries of the Apocalypse are progressively unsealed, the full implications of the Lordship of Christ over *all* creation will become increasingly manifest. And we will discover that in coming to Christ, to the *one* Lord, we are also coming "to the city of the living God, the Heavenly Jerusalem, and to innumerable angels in festal gathering" (Hb. 12:22).

4

Cum Angelis et Archangelis

TWO PRINCIPAL IMAGES ARE USED IN Scripture to describe the angels *collectively:* 1) choirs of singers and musicians; and 2) hosts of warriors. Love and war again. We speak of the nine choirs, ordered in three Rings about God and his plan. We speak also of the heavenly hosts, drawn up in battle array to execute the divine judgments, avenge the offended majesty of God and assist the struggling Church on earth. We have already considered the angels' combative offices. It remains to examine the choirs.

It is significant that Scripture and Tradition do not call the angels "intelligences" but rather prefer the titles of singers and warriors. The nine "academies" of angels would not quite do, even metaphorically. To be sure, they are intelligent! But their knowledge is not academic or "brainy." It is a knowledge of vision, yes, but of a *beatific* vision — that is, one that makes you deeply and overwhelmingly *happy*. And such knowledge does not evoke mere intellectual assent, nor is it entirely requited by a simple, assertive *amen*. We are closer to the truth when we imagine this knowledge as evoking an explosion of song, something that leaks into the physical world every time we hear a lovely passage of Gregorian Chant, of Renaissance madrigals, of Bach's fugues, or any number of phrases of great music from Beethoven to Bruckner.

The nine choirs of angels are comparable to nine choruses, nine ringing and harmonically rich choirs of tenors, sopranos and basses in duets, trios, solos and counterpoints undreamt of by the great masters. And even — to give full vent to our figurative language — instruments! Violins, cymbals, drums, trumpets, the likes of which we have never seen. As inadequate as such allegories are, they suggest angelic reality far more realistically than would a gallery of graduated light bulbs.

So, the angels sing. Scripture does not lay out the ordering of the nine choirs in explicit terms. Like so many matter-of-fact beliefs in the cultural world of the Jews and early Christians, it was perhaps too obvious a truth to merit separate elaboration. Here again, the oral tradition deposits itself in Scripture only according to need. The choirs are referred to in passing, this or that choir or group of choirs selected as most illustrative of the point to be made. The very ease of these references, however, betrays a clear, underlying angelology.

There are slightly different listings of the choirs among the Fathers and other theologians and spiritual writers of the Christian tradition (and indeed of the Jewish and Muslim traditions as well). Highly detailed knowledge of the angels is not given to us in this life. However, the great majority — from the author known as Dionysius the Areopagite and St. Gregory the Great to St. Hildegard of Bingen, Thomas Aquinas and Dante — hold to the number nine. It is reasonable to conclude that additional groupings numbered by some can be reduced to sub-divisions, or task-related formations of a temporary nature, of the basic nine choirs.

Excursus I: *On Dionysius the Areopagite*

It is worth pausing a bit to consider the credentials of the theologian most credited with the nine-choir division. A man of this name was a well-known jurist in Athens during St. Paul's visit to the city. He was famously converted by the Apostle (Acts 17). A group of four books attributed to him appeared during the Middle Ages and became the go-to source for the enumeration of the nine choirs, their names and functions. There seems to have been little question among medieval authors (including Thomas Aquinas) that the works were written by the Athenian convert. Understandably, they thus bore a quasi-Apostolic authority. In modern times, however, the detection of strong Neoplatonic influence (especially from Proclus, a 5th-century Platonist) led scholars to reject the 1st-century authorship; most saw the origin of the books in 5th- or 6th-century Syria, probably by a writer seeking readership by false attribution, or quite possibly a fraud.

In recent years, however, the body of texts has received more favorable assessments. To begin with, it has been pointed out that modern categories of intellectual property and copyright did not exist in ancient and medieval times. Attributing a work to an earlier authority could be a sign of humility rather than fraud, and the ideas contained therein considered as truly deriving from earlier sources, even if passing through subsequent generations and editions. Neoplatonic influence, particularly in what regards triadic structures, are abundantly present in St. Augustine's *De Trinitate* and other works of the Fathers. Furthermore, the notion that the millions of angels are just a mass of individuals, and do not belong to groupings that in some way reflect the Triune God, would be a bit unusual, to say the least. One could suspect even a touch of nominalism in this (orphaned, "classless" individuals), but certainly anachronism.[1]

---

1 "It must also be recognized that 'forgery' is a modern notion. Like Plotinus and the Cappadocians before him, Dionysius does not claim to be an innovator, but rather a communicator of a tradition. Adopting

That the first four choirs are the Seraphim, the Cherubim, the Thrones and the Dominations, and the last two the Archangels and the Angels, is supported by virtually all sources. Scripture and the liturgy leave little doubt about them. The greater Old Testament familiarity with the first two choirs, and the relative clarity of all five names, has facilitated their identification. The fifth, sixth and seventh choirs, however, are mentioned only in composite lists in the Epistles, and all have names denoting, in Greek, some kind of power or authority. This has led to variations in the specification of their proper works and inspired different sequences for ordering them. But even human groupings inevitably produce ambiguities. Do the English live in Britain, Great Britain, the UK or England? Is the country of the Burmese Burma or Myanmar?

Commonly, the names used for these three choirs are transla-tions from three Greek terms used in the New Testament, and are usually rendered in English as the Powers, the Principalities and the Virtues. Exactly how one orders the *names* is rather arbitrary. If, however, there were some principle of hierarchy that would

the persona of an ancient figure was a long established rhetorical device (known as *declamatio*), and others in Dionysius's circle also adopted pseud-onymous names from the New Testament. Dionysius's works, therefore, are much less a forgery in the modern sense than an acknowledgement of reception and transmission, namely, a kind of coded recognition that the resonances of any sacred undertaking are intertextual, bringing the diachronic structures of time and space together in a synchronic way, and that this theological teaching, at least, is dialectically received from another. Dionysius represents his own teaching as coming from a certain Hierotheus and as being addressed to a certain Timotheus. He seems to conceive of himself, therefore, as an in-between figure, very like a Dionysius the Areopagite, in fact. Finally, if Iamblichus and Proclus can point to a pri-mordial, pre-Platonic wisdom, namely, that of Pythagoras, and if Plotinus himself can claim not to be an originator of a tradition (after all, the term Neoplatonism is just a convenient modern tag), then why cannot Dionysius point to a distinctly Christian theological and philosophical resonance in an earlier pre-Plotinian wisdom that instantaneously bridged the gap between Judaeo-Christianity (St. Paul) and Athenian paganism (the Are-opagite)?" *Stanford Encycl. of Philosophy*, online: https://plato.stanford.edu/entries/pseudo-dionysius-areopagite/#SouIdeTer (referenced 04/21/2021).

help to correlate these three with the other, better-known choirs, we might find the key to assigning the most fitting denominations.

Fortunately, many Scriptural and linguistic pointers give us a close enough understanding of the higher three and lower two choirs that a kind of vertical ordering criterion can be identified and followed. The Thrones have a name that suggests they are the "steady, established" angels who support life and serve as the bases for the structures of creation; thus, their "paternal" qualities suggest association with the Father (after all, fathers *support* their families). The Cherubim, so related to the word in the Old Testament, suggest association with the Son, who is the Word in Person. The Seraphim, finally, whose name means "the burning ones"—thus making them, in a special way, angels of love—would logically be correlated with the Holy Spirit.

Looking to the last two choirs, the Archangels would appear to stand beneath the Cherubim, for they are constantly bearing words from God to man (St. Michael and St. Gabriel foremost among them); they also evince the same dynamic quality as do the angels of the second choir. The ninth choir of Angels (for whom the generic name becomes a proper choir name), being the group closest to man, is commonly considered to be the choir of guardian angels, whose task is first and foremost that of *guarding* our lives. Accordingly, they seem to logically stand under the influence of the Thrones with whom they share the custodianship of life.

The Seraphim, as we saw, are the highest, sovereign choir in the first Ring. They are also the angels of love. Charity is the highest of the virtues, and love is identified by St. John with the very being of God (1 Jn. 4:8). It would appear fitting that the choirs especially ordered to the Holy Spirit, and thus to love, would be the highest choir in each Ring. As the Archangels and Angels of the third Ring are already ordered to the Son and the Father respectively, the seventh choir would be ordered to the Spirit. And as the Angels guard our lives, and the Archangels bring us the word and point to the Sacraments of the Son (the traditional numbering of the "*Seven* Archangels"—testified in art and literary references—suggests a relationship to the seven Sacraments), the seventh choir may well be charged with our perfection in virtue, especially the virtue of charity. This would suggest giving them precisely the name of Virtues.

That leaves the Powers and Principalities. When one considers the hierarchy of the Son from the Cherubim down to the Archangels, the very dynamism of this stream of grace suggests the word "Powers" as the best name for the fifth choir. "The word of God is living and active, sharper than any two-edged sword" (Hb. 4:12). Likewise, it is not difficult to fit the name of "Principalities," or "Princes," with its obvious "administrative" connotation, into the work of the 6th choir. They would stand with the choirs of Thrones and Angels, who support and protect life respectively. This would leave to the Princes the task of ordering and stewarding that same life, particularly in the broader cosmic context.

The fourth choir—almost by default—would have to be the Dominations, standing in the channel of love extending from the Seraphim to the Virtues. If, as we shall see presently, the upper three choirs are turned to the "court" of God, and the three lower choirs to our earth, the three middle choirs are understood by Dionysius to administer the whole of the cosmic creation. Could it be that the Dominations possess the attractive power of love, and that this also "dominates" the universe through this highest of the three middle choirs? One might even wonder if universal gravitation could be a physical manifestation of this power. Here we can only conjecture.

Beginning with the Church Fathers, then taken up by Dionysius and later theologians in a systematic way, a division of the nine choirs into three "ternaries," or "rings," has become traditional. A further Trinitarian reflection is evident here. Holy Scripture speaks often of a three-fold hierarchy which may well be the Rings of the angelic choirs. For instance, in Deuteronomy 10:14, we read: "Behold, to the Lord your God belong [1] heaven, and [2] the *heaven of heavens*, [3] the *earth* with all that is in it" (cf. 1 Kings 8:27; Neh. 9:6). The heaven of heavens would be the inner court of the Most Holy Trinity, where the Seraphim sing their praises (Is. 6). And they are turned, as are all the angels of this Ring, entirely toward the glory of him who is *"enthroned* upon the Cherubim" (Ps. 79:2). The "fiery ones" "enthroned" upon the "word."

The angels of the lower three choirs, standing at the other pole of the hierarchy, would be turned in a special way toward human beings and the Church on earth. Are not the ninth choir of guardian angels and the eighth choir of Archangels already directly occupied with man-related tasks?

When Einstein famously quipped that the most miraculous feature of the cosmos was its *intelligibility*, he might have profited from a deeper knowledge of angelology than Spinoza's philosophy could afford. When defenders of arguments for the existence of God point to the intelligible structure of physical reality and our ability to map it onto our rational and mathematical schemes, they enjoy pointing to an intelligent being behind it all, i.e., God. Albeit granting God's ultimate causality, it would be even more helpful to point not just to his intelligence, but to the intelligences (plural) created by him to administer his complex creation.

Excursus 2: *How central is our earth?*

When referring to the upper angelic choirs as centered on God Most High — and thus ultimately transcending physical reality — and the middle choirs as distributed over the vast cosmic creation, and then the lower choirs, like the higher, also centered, but this time on our earth, a few words should be said about the classical geocentric view of the universe. Competing models have always existed in one form or the other. In modern times the heliocentric view, and later the a-centric view, have become the common way of viewing our world's situation and position in the broader universe. How might such modern astrophysics square with the orders of angels as presented here?

Christian doctrine has nothing definitive to say about the trillion galaxies in our cosmos, or whether there could even be intelligent life on some planet beyond our earth. The faith only insists that it is all a part of God's creation. The Biblical story centers quite obviously upon our earth. It is the drama that unfolds *here* that is of interest; accordingly, the story as such is necessarily geocentric, whatever astrophysics might add in context and measurement.

Nonetheless, beyond this framework of human creation and redemption, there is another sense in which the geocentric model is unavoidable. Whatever sophisticated astronomical science may teach about galaxies and stars, it will be largely a view derived from abstractions made from telescopic observation and also the careful measurement of electromagnetic radiation of various types. Outside of the extremely rare occurrence of a supernova, the sighting of a meteor, or the more regular movements of sun, moon and planets, our view of the cosmos is a static view. And since science is now convinced that no particular point of reference is normative according to purely scientific criteria, a favored perspective meaningfully determined by a non-scientific viewpoint cannot be discarded out of hand. We should remember that before satellite navigation, all the ships in the world plotted their courses on the basis of a geocentric worldview. And, winds and waves permitting, they got to their destinations.

We live, on a day-to-day basis, in the world revealed by our five unaided senses. We do not live experientially among atoms or molecules, or next to pulsars or black holes. And for those of us who believe that the world was created by divine design, and that we were placed within it according to a transcendent artwork we only imperfectly understand, the way it looks to our eyes without microscopes or telescopes will always have priority over the more intrusive squints of modern science. Even the scientists can only peek through those cutting-edge instruments if they have eyepieces proportioned to their physical eyeballs. Einstein himself still drank coffee and walked on two legs after filling a blackboard with all the arcane mathematics of relativity physics.

It has become a common theme in contemporary philosophy of science, and even of science fiction, that the world that is disclosed by our high-tech instruments is hardly a hospitable dwelling for our race. We look in vain for signs of meaning, value or purpose in quantum mechanics, relativity theory or even — I would be willing to assert — in the human genome. Those signs we only find in a world in which the earth beneath us appears to be motionless and the stars above us a dependable, revolving backdrop. This is the world the Bible speaks of, and also the world our everyday experience testifies to. This does not come from antiquated "medieval" geocentrism but simply from our experience of the real world in which we live and die. The discovery that angelic reality takes its bearings from this perspective makes perfect sense.

Excursus 3: *What about the "others"?*

By the others I mean the fallen spirits (about which much remains to be said in the second part of this book), as well as the world of subtle and spiritual beings presented in other traditions. The Christian tradition leaves little doubt about the particularity and uniqueness of Christ and his work. A consequence of this is also the uniqueness and normative structure, if I may put it thus, of the choirs of the holy angels. And in the Christian view of reality, being holy also means being maximally *real*.

The fallen angels have *fallen away from* God and thus have also *fallen out of* his holy order. They are to this extent *less* real. As they nonetheless pretend at times to be angels of light and to emulate the holy angels, they will "hang around" the choirs to which they once belonged. They will be unable, however, to get a full grip on principles they no longer obey. The "war in heaven" we have already referred to is Scripture's way of characterizing this uneasy coexistence of holy and fallen angels, at least until the *Parousia* (Second Coming).

As for the throngs of spiritual and subtle creatures described, named and often worshipped in other traditions, the Christian has only two options for understanding their reality and work. On the one hand, often enough it will be the case of one epiphany or another of fallen angels who succeed in gaining for themselves attention, and even adoration. This is especially so where such spirits require cults of unnatural practices, gruesome sacrifices or where hideous ugliness is involved. In other cases — particularly where admirable and even virtuous traits are presented in a given culture's lore regarding its gods — we may well have a more complex picture before us.

We know from the history of the world's literature and mythology how powerful an instrument the human imagination can be in creating worlds of parallel realities. *The Lord of the Rings, Harry*

Potter and *Star Wars* are cases in point. When we move, however, into the complex angelologies and demonologies of ancient Egypt and Mesopotamia, or of the Andean and Meso-American hierarchies of spirits, and even more of the rich traditions of *devas, avataras, buddhas, bodhisattvas* and other supernal beings witnessed to in the vast mythologies of South Asia and the Far East — we are deluded if we deem them to be nothing but figments of overcharged phantasies, wishful thinking or longings of the human heart. There is simply too much that rings true, and too many documentations of preternatural occurrences to simply dismiss them as pure fiction.

Furthermore, a bit closer to home, when we ponder the Olympian gods of Greece and their later Roman versions, we find ourselves still naming cars after them and admiring their statues in museums throughout the world. Apollo and Minerva, for instance, seem somehow more like old friends than fire-breathing demons, even to Christians.

We should remember that the ancient Greeks and Romans themselves were not entirely sure what to make of their long-held belief in the gods. Popular belief abounded, but intellectual skeptics were also not hard to find. Men as wise as Plato and Aristotle chose not to express serious doubts as to their existence. Even sober old Cicero reveals his own perplexity about all this in his famous treatise *On the Nature of the Gods*.

From a Christian perspective, the best approach to the vast lore of non-Biblical, non-Christian spiritual beings — beyond the clear demarcation of the fallen angels — is probably to attribute the details to an ultimately unresolvable amalgam of three factors: 1) genuine survivals of a primordial wisdom about the world of God and his spirits, many dimensions of which are true and noble; 2) the addition of demonic influence and confusion, where the guidance of God's definitive revelation is unavailable; and 3) a generous input of pure human imagination, motivated by desire, hope, fear and any number of other inspirations.

We thus arrive at the following arrangement of the nine choirs of angels, employing both the horizontal triadic principle of the three Rings and the vertical principle of the three Persons of the Holy Trinity:

	SPIRIT (LOVE)	SON (WORD)	FATHER (LIFE)
1st Ring	I. Seraphim	II. Cherubim	III. Thrones
2nd Ring	IV. Dominations	V. Powers	VI. Princes
3rd Ring	VII. Virtues	VIII. Archangels	IX. Angels

Though the names may vary, the tasks we are identifying as belonging to the fifth and sixth choirs correspond perfectly with the attributes assigned to these choirs by Dionysius. He attributes to the fifth choir a "virile" and "inflexible" quality, well evoked by the name "Power" and conveying the essential dynamism of the spoken word. This name is given to the fifth choir already by St. John Damascene. To the sixth choir, Dionysius attributes "order" and "harmony," squaring well with the life-ordering and quasi-governmental work of a choir identified as "Princes."

St. Gregory the Great already gave the name of "Virtues" to the seventh choir (see Appendix). Dante Alighieri, in his *Paradiso*, has Dionysius smile to himself as St. Gregory enters heaven, for he differed from him in the names he gave to the choirs (*Paradiso* Canto 28). This should perhaps advise us to heed St. Thomas Aquinas's admonition that the wise man does not quarrel about names. Once we have found cogent reasons for a nomenclature, the rest is convention.

Every day, before the Church crosses the threshold of that most sublime, Seraphic prayer of the *Sanctus*, entering thereby into the awesome mystery of the Holy Sacrifice, she reverently pauses and prays a long and poetic Preface. Here, as in no other official liturgical prayer, she requires that her children explicitly invoke the choirs of angels by name, and only dare to sing their song after having humbly petitioned their help: "*Cum Angelis et Archangelis . . .*" (with angels and archangels...). What more proof do we need that we are one family with these nine choirs of pure spirits and should endeavor to pass ever more deeply through their multiple mysteries, as if through the nine mystical months of our own nativity in Christ?

5

Our Three-Part Drama

NOTHER TRINITARIAN LIGHT FALLS upon our lives in the actual unfolding of our story. We know the great importance of history in the working out of the mystery of Christ. Our Lord was born in time, indeed in the "fullness of time," and founded a Church which was to endure through the rest of human history. This was to be the organ for mediating the saving graces of his Redemption. On the other side of that watershed, the entire Old Testament shows us the long, struggling history of man and of the Chosen People before the advent of Christ. Judeo-Christian revelation reveals God. But it reveals God by inserting divine agencies and graces into terrestrial time, allowing our all-too-human story to become a vehicle of providential communications.

This drama is presented to us in the Bible. It is no secret that the Old Testament is in the first instance a revelation of the mystery of the Father, and that the Gospels reveal to us the Son. It is furthermore clear that beginning with Pentecost at the opening of the Acts of the Apostles and culminating in the Apocalypse, it is the workings of the Holy Spirit that stand in the foreground. We thus see a Trinitarian principle at work in the three major chronological steps of sacred history: Genesis (beginning), Gospel (climax) and Apocalypse (end).

We are wise to avoid separating these dimensions too rigorously or assigning dates to an "era of the Spirit," as has been incautiously attempted in the past. The general scheme of the three steps, however, is evident and essential to sketching even an approximate outline of salvation history. Just as Christ did not come to abolish the Old Testament but to fulfill it, likewise the Spirit comes to perfect the work of Christ, and not to supersede it.

We may put the matter as follows: In the Old Testament, the Father stands in the foreground as the Creator and Lord, awe-inspiring, holy and almighty; the Son remains in the background as the promised

Messiah yet to come, whereas the Spirit serves as the inspiration of the prophets who point to that very Advent. As we open the pages of the Gospels, however, at once we see the figure of the God-Man, the Son Incarnate, stepping into the foreground as the Messiah and Savior. Here the Father is the one who steps into the background, but now for the first time fully *as* the Father. Jesus taught us to call God our Father. Furthermore, rather than the Son, now it is the Spirit who is the promised one, the Paraclete to be sent by both the Father and the Son.

Once the Paraclete is sent on Pentecost, it is he who stands in the foreground, guiding the Church and filling her members with the graces won by the Redemption. Christ himself, however, now steps back from his visible ministry, turning that over to his Apostles and their successors: the bishops and priests, and with them all the people of God. He steps back and assumes his quiet throne in the tabernacle. In this last phase, beginning with Pentecost and ending with the *Parousia*, the Father remains in the background, but now not only as Creator and Father but also, henceforth, as *Goal*—as he *to whom* we journey. In the Lord's Prayer as in the Mass, it is *to* the Father that we typically direct our prayers, for he is the final station of our pilgrimage and the ultimate recipient of our worship.

Now it is by understanding the special work of the angels in each of these three stages of sacred history that we arrive at a proper evaluation of their role in the Church today. We have already seen how closely they are related to the mystery of Christ in the Gospels. They are the humble, serving spirits, ministering to the Incarnate God. They look on in astonishment as God walks among men, and as he plants the Cross firmly in the soil of our earth. In the Gospel, once they have performed their ministries, they step into the background, making way for the awesome figure of the God-Man Jesus Christ.

But this singular posture of the angels during Our Lord's time on earth was new, differing both from their Old Testament situation and from the new role into which they would increasingly grow after the descent of the Spirit. Let us look back briefly on the work of the angels in the Old Covenant.

Accustomed as we are to a soft and effeminate portrayal of the angels, we are likely to find the angelic figures of the Old Testament a bit intimidating. Often enough, the first words out of their mouths when they appear to humans are: "Be not afraid!" There was good reason to forewarn us. The sudden invasion of pure spirit into our dense and dark world of corporeal reality can have the effect of a lightning bolt.

They were the first to be created, identified simply as the "heavens," as "light." But already in the trial of man, the presence of the fallen spirits became evident, and our first parents found themselves immediately placed in a moral predicament. The Tempter used all his tricks to seduce Adam and Eve into following the vanguard of the demons, and to convince them "not to keep their own position but leave their proper dwelling" (Jude v. 6), and to "ascend above the heights of the clouds, and make themselves like the Most High" (Is. 14:14).

The attempt to conquer the Tree of Knowledge represents the fundamental pride of the creature who insists on "knowing" before obeying and loving. We already bristle as small children when told to mind our parents, for our earnest "why?" is greeted with what seems a most unsatisfactory rationale: "Because I said so." But it was in truth very satisfactory. If children obeyed only when their minds could get a purchase on the ways of the world, very few humans would ever hit puberty. Obedience puts us on the safe pathway of probable survival. Knowledge will come soon enough.

Through this inaugural act of humility, a fruit of love was supposed to grow in the hearts of the first angels and of the first human beings. By means of their free and trusting submission to the mysterious will of God, their hearts would have opened in love, and precisely through this initiation of the will, their minds open in knowledge.

This fruit of love is born of the first sacrifice: the sacrifice of the intellect. God can never be "figured out" by those he creates, any more than an artisan can be figured out by the artefacts he makes. Even if the *Mona Lisa* had a brain, she would never understand Leonardo. A creature must first acknowledge the absolute sovereignty of the Creator in all things, and that includes especially those that surpass its understanding. Only in the aftermath of that surrender can God fill the intellect with knowledge, and then with the peace that passes all understanding. Only then can God pour the fullness of his life into the soul and invite that soul to bathe in everlasting glory.

In order that man not approach the other inviting Tree of Life, gain immortality and thus perpetuate his sin like that of the fallen angels, God turns to the second choir of angels. Man is driven from the Garden, and holy Cherubim, the highest angels of the word, are stationed at the gates. Back he goes to the soil from which he was originally taken (the ungraced and now wounded state of nature, Gn. 3:23). A flaming sword of God's purest, *now unbearable* Word is flourished by the Cherubim, "turning every way, to guard the way to the Tree of Life" (Gn. 3:24). Learning to endure that Word without pain is one way of describing the whole process of our salvation and sanctification.

The "Four Living Creatures" of Ezekiel (Ezek. 1) have traditionally been identified with the Cherubim, or angels at the level of the Cherubim (who also return in Apoc. 4). The eye of faith has also discerned these Creatures to be present in the message of the four Gospels, symbolized in Christian art by a Man, a Lion, an Ox and an Eagle.

In this way, the sword turning in all directions in Genesis, and the Creatures facing all directions in Ezekiel, morph into the four-fold revelation of the Gospel, *going out* in all directions, "into all the world" (Mk. 16:15). There it will be the Word that is Christ, encompassed by the words of the Evangelists, and it will go forth indeed, but no longer to ward off, like a centrifuge, but rather to gather everyone in with centripetal love. That force of love will draw all things to himself (Jn. 12:32) and finally welcome the prodigal son home. The Cherubs' threatening sword of repulsion will become the healing Rood of Christ.

So it is that in the Old Testament, the holy angels of God are already guardians. But it is not only man who is guarded, but even more the holy things of God. The angels will fight. They will at times guide (see the book of Tobit). Indeed, it is they who will lead Israel into the Promised Land. But their overriding concern, discernible in nearly every book of the Old Testament, is to serve and avenge the majesty of God Almighty.

To be sure, they also live up to their name "angel," which in Greek simply means messenger *(angelos)*. "The Angel of the Lord" appears frequently in Scripture, and often merely communicates the divine decrees. We see this with the angel who visited Hagar, Abraham's handmaid, foretelling the birth of Ishmael (Gn. 16).

Three angels then visit Abraham, by the Oaks of Mamre. They first are seen as "three men," but at the end of the passage as the Lord himself. This presents us, in miniature, both the angels' typical assumption of human form in order to communicate with us, and also their ultimate task, which is only to be couriers of the Lord. In this case, they bring Abraham the news of his aged wife's impending pregnancy. Thereafter, they "looked toward Sodom," and mediate the famous "bargaining transaction" between the Lord and Abraham as to the minimal demographics of the good that need to reside in the sinful city in order to avert divine judgment. Abraham gets it from 50 down to 10, but apparently that minimum was not reached. Here we are taught that we should pray indeed, as God can be moved by our petitions; but there are limits (Gn. 18).

In the following chapter, when two angels come to visit Lot (Gn. 19), their "message" exemplifies the more common Old Testament angelic task. Referring to the wicked city of Sodom, they declare: "We are about to destroy this place, because the outcry against its people has become great before the Lord, and the Lord has sent us to destroy it" (Gn. 19:13).

It was an angel who stayed the arm of Abraham as he was about to sacrifice his own son. This angelic act expressed the divine acceptance of the sacrifice Abraham had just made of both intellect and will to his God, but also God's rejection henceforth of all human sacrifice (Gn. 22). From that day on, if ever a human sacrifice was to be made, it would be God himself who would allow it, and indeed make the offering himself. "For God so loved the world that he gave his one and only Son . . ." (cf. John 3:16).

Abraham's grandson, Jacob, whose vision of the heaven's ladder we have already touched upon, has another extraordinary encounter with the angels. It evokes a further exclamation from the patri-arch: "Jacob went on his way and the angels of God met him; and when Jacob saw them he said, 'This is God's army!'" (Gn. 32:1-2).

Shortly thereafter, he wrestles with "a man" all night long (Gn. 32), later identified as God but usually depicted in sacred art as an angel, and the spirit, unable to prevail against him, touches the "hollow of his thigh." Thus was sanctified that current of life which was to issue from Jacob's loins as the Twelve Tribes. And on the same occasion he receives the name "Israel" (meaning "one who struggles with God") and is blessed. But Jacob senses that this is no "man," and wants to know who he is. The mysterious figure, having completed his task by testing the strength of the patriarch, promptly withdraws and refuses to disclose his name.

The prophets Elijah and Elisha seem to have lived with angels as much as with men. We recall the angel who came and woke a despondent Elijah, prompting him to fulfill his vocation (1 Kings 19:4–8). But perhaps the most impressive scene was when Elisha was surrounded in Dothan by the Syrian army; his servant began to tremble, and Elisha prayed to the Lord to open the servant's eyes, "and behold, the mountain was full of horses and chariots of fire round about Elisha" (2 Kings 6:17). As with Jacob before, Elisha too is granted the special grace of seeing the throngs of angels who are always there but seldom perceived.

The Book of Psalms refers frequently to the holy angels. Psalm 33, for example, sings: "The angel of the Lord encamps around those who fear him and delivers them." And Psalm 90: "He will give his angels charge of you, to guard you in all your ways. On their hands they will bear you up, lest you dash your foot against a stone." As elsewhere in the Old Testament, so also in its book of hymns, the angels of God are unmistakably present.

As we move into the books of the prophets, and attention to the coming of the Messiah grows more pronounced, the angels join the prophets in looking forward to this unfolding design of their inscrutable God. The great Isaiah is prepared for his mission by a member of the highest choir, the Seraphim (Is. 6). He is shown a vision of the Lord upon a throne, and the Seraphim singing one to another the classic prayer of praise, the *Sanctus*. Then, one of them flies to him with a burning coal from the fiery altar of God's love and purifies the lips of the prophet. Now he can begin to speak of Christ. In this way the lips which (in the following chapter) will prophecy that "a virgin shall conceive and bear a son" were first singed by the burning ardor of the highest of God's angels.

As we get closer to the fullness of time, however, the images of the angels begin to grow more familiar and approachable. Already with Daniel, we are introduced for the first time to angels of the third Ring, the Archangels St. Gabriel (Dan. 8) and St. Michael (10). And in the book of Tobit, we have the story of the third Biblical Archangel, St. Raphael, and his escorting and medicinal ministries to Tobias. This brings the work of guardian angels into a new profile.

The commanding, august works of the upper choirs seem to grow quiet as the Incarnation approaches. It is as if they had all been gazing heavenwards for millennia in rapt adoration of God the Son, when suddenly that very Son descended before their eyes like a high diver into the depths of the earth. The most sublime of all God's creatures find themselves stunned as they witness, almost in disbelief, the self-emptying of the exalted God they so adore.

In the fullness of time, the angels reverently serve Our Lord and watch the cosmic drama suddenly focus entirely on the salvation of this third creature called man. We have already seen how intimately the angels are involved in the key events of Our Lord's life. Their involvement, however, was that of servants and messengers, not that of protagonists. After Christ's Ascension and the sending of the Holy Spirit, the third great phase of the Biblical story commences. The angels will begin to step in new and surprising ways onto the scene of salvation.

We know that two of the four Evangelists wrote another book in addition to their Gospels. St. Luke wrote the Acts of the Apostles, and St. John is traditionally considered the author of the Apocalypse. Both the Acts and the Apocalypse are sequels to the Gospels, the first presenting the immediate consequences of the sending of the Holy Spirit, and the last presenting the ultimate consequences of that mission. The Acts—describing the early establishment of the Church as it began in Jerusalem with the Jews (Acts 1) and ended in Rome with the Gentiles (Acts 28)—can be divided into two major parts. The first focuses on the figure of St. Peter (Acts 1–12); the second, on the figure of St. Paul (Acts 13–28).

St. Peter is the Rock upon whom Christ willed to found his Church (Mt. 16:18). For Catholics, he is the first pope, the foundational and fatherly figure to whom is entrusted the stewardship of the life of the Church. St. Paul, on the other hand, is more a rocket than a rock. The radical difference between the two is clear; but so is the need of every rocket to have a solid, unmoving launch pad from which to take off. So St. Paul takes off and conquers the world. He is the Apostle not so much of the Father and of life, as is St. Peter, but rather of the Son and of the Word. Thus, the Acts of the Apostles recount the *acts* of the paternal, groundwork mission of Peter, and of the filial, dynamic mission of Paul. *Both* are formative of the life of the nascent church.

Since man is by nature ordered to the Son and to the Word, the work of St. Paul is by far the most active, and even the most human. We find in the second half of the Acts relatively little intervention on the part of the angels. He once refers to "an angel of the God to whom I belong" as assuring him and his travel companions of a safe

52

trip (Acts 27:23−24). Also, the "man of Macedonia" who appears to him in a vision, bidding him to cross from Asia into Macedonia to help them (Acts 16:9−10), is interpreted by many commentators as an angel. The angels seem to have an eye on the universal mission of the Church even before the Apostles. After all, St. Peter awoke to this fact as an angelic protagonist "arranged" his meeting with the Roman Cornelius (cf. Acts 10). Likewise, it is angelic GPS that directs the Apostle St. Philip to turn south in order to encounter an Ethiopian he was ordained to convert (Acts 8:26−40).

When St. Thomas Aquinas wrote his commentary on 2 Corinthians, he pondered the intriguing passage in chapter 12 about St. Paul being "caught up to the third heaven . . . caught up into Paradise . . . [where he] heard things that cannot be told, which man may not utter" (2 Cor. 12:2−4). Aquinas surmised the Apostle had been lifted temporarily into the First Ring of the angels and was able to see what they see (*In II Cor.* 12, lect. 1; n. 454).

Turning back to the first half of the Acts, we flip through twelve chapters and count the angelic aids to St. Peter as he labors to lay the foundations of the Church. After that initial apparition of the two angels following Christ's Ascension (Acts 1:10−11), it is not long before the first Vicar of Christ is guided by God's angels (Acts 5:19−20; 10:3ff.; 12:23). And of the first deacon we hear that St. Stephen's "face was like the face of an angel" as he approached his death (Acts 6:15). As this first martyr of Christianity gives his last address, he mentions the angels, good and bad, no less than six times (Acts 7).

The most significant angelic event of all, of course, occurs when St. Peter is freed from prison by "an angel of the Lord," is told to "get up quickly," "dress yourself and put on your sandals," and "wrap your mantle around you and *follow me.*" Poor Peter thinks he is seeing a vision, until the Iron Gate leading to the city opens of itself and suddenly his mysterious deliverer vanishes. The first bishop of Rome exclaims: "Now I am sure that the Lord has sent his angel and rescued me from the hand of Herod and from all that the Jewish people were expecting" (Acts 12).

When St. Peter appears at the house of Mary, mother of John Mark, the maid answers the door and then announces his presence to the family. Not yet aware that he was released by an angel, they conclude that the person standing at the door must be one! "It is his angel!" they respond in chorus. This would seem to bear witness to the matter-of-fact acceptance of angels as personal guardians among early Christians. Later in this same chapter, old Herod, who had imprisoned St. Peter to begin with, was lapping up the adulation of his subjects when "an angel of the Lord smote him, because he did not give God the glory; and he was eaten by worms and died" (Acts 12:23). Even in the New Testament, the angels have their abrupt moments.

Now just as St. Peter and St. Paul stand ordered to the Father and Son in their respective Apostolic Acts — all of which is recorded in St. Luke's second book — the third of the three most prominent Apostles stands very much in the mystery of the Spirit of love. When we turn to the Apocalypse, we do not find the "acts" of an Apostle. As a matter of fact, St. John does not really *do* much of anything at all. He just looks. "After this I looked, and lo, in heaven an open door!" (Apoc. 4:1) "In the Spirit" (Apoc. 4:2), he looks and sees the throne of God, and afterwards, he watches the angels work. For fifteen chapters, he watches, as the angels work. This book is not at all about further acts of Apostles. One might even rename it the "Acts of the Angels." It is to this book, and to our present situation in salvation history, that we must now turn.

6

Vatican II and the Angels

POPE ST. JOHN XXIII IS FAMOUS FOR PLAN-
ning and convening the 21st Ecumenical Council of the
Church, known to us as Vatican II. Pope John is also known
for something else: he was extremely devoted to his guardian angel.
We have already mentioned the importance given by his successor,
St. Paul VI, to the reality of the angels. We shall now take a look
at the famous council itself, presided over by both, and discover
the angels to be present as in perhaps no other of all the Church's
councils.

The Pastoral Constitution on the Liturgy places the mystery of
the Church's official prayer in explicit relationship to the praise
offered by the heavenly choristers. Once again, they are depicted
both as soldiers and as singers:

"In the earthly liturgy we take part in a foretaste of that heavenly
liturgy which is celebrated in the Holy City of Jerusalem toward
which we journey as pilgrims, where Christ is sitting at the right
hand of God, Minister of the true tabernacle. With all the warriors of the heavenly army we sing a hymn of glory to the Lord"
(*Sacrosanctum Concilium*, n. 8).

As already mentioned, the Church requires that we call upon
the choirs of angels before we commence the Eucharistic Prayer

of the Mass. And in the first of those prayers, just after the Consecration, the Angel of the Lord is explicitly called upon by the
priest to "carry this sacrifice to [God's] altar in heaven." Furthermore, in the liturgical reform following the Council, the Church
has wisely judged to keep two traditional feasts in honor of the
angels. October 2nd remains the memorial in honor of all guardian
angels. But there is another.

The 29th of September has long been a day of the angels, and
especially of St. Michael. That the key role of the angels might be
even more manifest, the otherwise separate commemorations of St.
Raphael (October 24) and St. Gabriel (March 24) have now been
joined to the day of St. Michael. Thus, through a feast honoring
the three Biblically named angels, all the hosts of heaven are honored at the altars of Christendom. A month before All (human)
Saints Day on November 1st, we now have an "All Angels Day."
Furthermore, one famous saint who was able to see her guardian
angel was St. Frances of Rome. Her feast day is still commemo-
rated on March 9th.

One motive for the simplification of the Church's universal
calendar after the council was to leave more room for provincial
feasts. There has been no dearth of locally inspired devotion to the
holy angels. The 8th of May is still observed in commemoration of
a famous apparition of St. Michael in southern Italy. John Paul II
visited this sanctuary on that feast day in 1987. A similar memorial
on October 16th marks the apparition of St. Michael on Mont
Tombe in France (now known as Mont St. Michel).

A Mass text in honor of the Seven Angels (cf. Apoc. 1:4) was
authorized by the pope in 1830 and was at one time celebrated
in some areas. Spain, Portugal and Brazil have had permission to
celebrate a proper feast in honor of each country's national guardian angel. In Portugal, for instance, the 10th of June is celebrated
as a memorial in honor of the "guardian angel of Portugal." To be
sure, the Church is always jealous of the centrality of Christ and
is rightly on guard lest a misdirected piety consume itself in a cult
of angels. St. Paul was acutely aware of the abuses here possible
(Col. 2:18). But only good things can be abused. To the extent
that one's love for the angels is like one's love for the saints — a

means of focusing and particularizing our love for Christ—it can no more obscure our view of the Lord than a focused eyepiece obscures your view of the stars.

For those who actually read the documents of Vatican II, the council's insistence on the place of the angels in the liturgy is clear and obvious. The Dogmatic Constitution on the Church speaks of the time "when the Lord will come in glory, and all his angels with him" (*Lumen Gentium*, n. 49), and of the fact that the Church has always venerated the saints, "together with the Blessed Virgin Mary and the holy angels, with a special love" (*Lumen Gentium*, n. 50). On the darker side of things, the careful reader of this council's documents will count at least eight explicit references to the devil and his angels (Appendix).

One need not obsess about the end of the world—the exact time of which we cannot know anyway (Mt. 24:36)—in order to point out the very evident signs of the times. Indeed, was it not the very purpose of Vatican II to read those signs and attempt to reposition the Church for its mission in a now largely secularized world? Reading those signs is a Christian obligation, enjoined upon us by Christ himself (cf. Mk. 13).

Just two years before he was elevated to the Chair of St. Peter, Karol Wojtyła spoke these words on a visit in the United States:

> We are now standing in the face of the greatest historical confrontation humanity has gone through. I do not think the wide circle of the Christian community realize this fully. We are now facing the final confrontation between the Church and the Antichrist, of the Gospel versus the Anti-Gospel. This confrontation lies within the plans of divine providence; it is a trial which the whole Church must take up.... (*The Wall Street Journal*, Nov. 9, 1978)

After becoming pope on October 16th, 1978, St. John Paul II repeatedly emphasized that we are in a decisive epoch of the Church's history. In the summer of 1986, in the midst of a series of catechetical addresses on the creed, the Holy Father came to the part of the creed that speaks of "things visible and invisible." *No less than six weekly catecheses were then delivered on the subject of angels*, far in excess of anything said about them by any previous pope. They have been published separately, and ought to be carefully read by all Christians (see Appendix).

Pope John Paul's visit to Fatima in May 1982, one year after his near assassination, confirms his support of the Fatima Message. It is significant that the little shepherds of Fatima experienced three angelic apparitions *before* the six apparitions of Our Lady. Nonetheless, Sr. Lucy did not speak publicly about them until after the authenticity of Mary's appearance had been proclaimed by the bishop of Fatima in 1930. The angel came before Mary, preparing the way, but preferred to step into the background thereafter.

The presence and power of the angel that appeared to the children of Fatima was so overwhelming that they felt exhausted after the apparition. The Virgin's apparitions, on the other hand, left them refreshed. So it was that Sr. Lucy hesitated before telling the world about the awesome presence of the holy angel at Fatima. First Mary's message had to ring out clearly.

Likewise, as we enter more deeply into the mysteries of the last book of the Bible, and the work of the angels, both holy and fallen, becomes more evident in the world and in the Church, we too will at first be hesitant to acknowledge their new profile. Our times are strange and frightening, but somehow pregnant with unprecedented promise. The Apocalypse is also a strange and frightening book. Still, in its pages, amidst all the battles and visitations it details, we witness the difficult birth of the New Jerusalem. These are the tensions, and this is the promise of the 21st century.

St. Padre Pio is said to have once affirmed: "I am convinced that this is the hour of the angels." And just five days before his death, Venerable Pius XII admonished a group of American pilgrims "to foster a certain familiar acquaintance with the angels, who are so constant in their solicitude for your salvation and holiness."

7

Our Lady's Subjects

THE FIRST TIME THE BIBLE BRINGS MARY into relationship with the world of angels is the sobering text in Genesis 3:15. Addressing the serpent, the Lord God says: "I will put enmity between you and the woman, between your seed and her seed; she shall crush your head, and you shall lie in wait of her heel." Christendom is full of pictures and statues portraying the humble Virgin standing with one of her delicate feet upon the serpentine head of the most powerful of God's creatures. As Mary herself sings in the Magnificat, "He has put down the mighty from their thrones and has exalted the lowly" (Lk. 1:52). We shall return to this dimension of the Virgin's presence in the second part of our book. Here we shall take a more comprehensive look at her role and her relation to the angels in the whole of salvation history.

As we saw previously, one of the first notable Old Testament prophecies of the Blessed Virgin was delivered by the prophet Isaiah just after having his lips purified by a Seraph (Is. 7:14). But just as Mary is the silent one in the New Testament, more pervasively present and eloquent through her silence than she could ever be through words, similarly, the Old Testament prophecies of her role in salvation are always clothed in mystery and metaphor. The eye of faith sees her coming prefigured in the cloud which so often envelops the presence of God in the time before Christ. "The glory of the Lord appeared in the cloud" (Ex. 16:10). "Then Moses went up on the mountain, and the cloud covered the mountain" (Ex. 24:15). "Then the Lord came down in the cloud and spoke to him" (Nb. 11:25). She whose humanity is to serve as the sacred veil of the Son's overwhelming divinity was already present in the figure of the cloud shielding man from the awful majesty of the Father.

Our Lady is also prefigured in the desert tabernacle, which bore the mystery of God's presence as she also would one day do. Every Christian altar reminds us of her, for it is upon the linens of the immaculate humanity she gives to Christ that the one true Sacrifice that saves the world is offered. In all these figurative ways, Mary's holy outline is progressively perceived in the pages of the Old Testament. But she is too closely entwined with the mystery of her Son to appear explicitly on the scene quite yet. His day was yet to come. The angels are only episodically conspicuous in the Old Covenant, for, like man, they too are still approaching both the mystery of Christ and the mystery of Mary.

But when she does appear in full reality for the first time in the pages of Scripture, we see her alone — alone with an angel. For centuries, this sole fact has commanded the attention of countless artists of Christendom. There is perhaps no more frequently portrayed scene in the whole of sacred history. We read of it in the opening chapter of St. Luke's Gospel, when the holy Archangel Gabriel "was sent from God to a city of Galilee named Nazareth, to a virgin betrothed to a man whose name was Joseph, of the house of David; and the virgin's name was Mary." God's great plan begins. And it begins with a meeting between an angel and a woman.

No quantity of words could increase the impact of this simple fact. No marshalling of theological argumentation could make any clearer the obvious and articulate message conveyed by the scene itself. An angel of God brings the most momentous and fateful message of all time: *the* Annunciation. And he brings it to a woman. The ensuing dialogue between the angel and the woman, in all its spontaneity and with all its drama, is so full of historical conse-quences for the life of every Christian that the Church has urged us to recite the one-act drama three times a day in the prayer of the Angelus:

> *"The Angel of the Lord declared unto Mary — and she conceived of the Holy Spirit."*

The message of the Father's will that his Son take on flesh in the womb of the Immaculate Virgin is delivered by St. Gabriel. This same Archangel was sent to Daniel in the Old Testament to help the prophet grasp the meaning of a vision: "Gabriel, make this man understand the vision" (Dn. 8:16). Here too, St. Gabriel must help the young maiden to understand the message. Her humility and her resolved virginity make the annunciation of her sublime maternal mission an immediate puzzle to her mind. The Archangel declares that she need not worry on either account, for it will be the Holy Spirit who will conceive in her. It will be his deed, not hers. The child shall be the only begotten Son of the Father, not the biological son of her husband. The angels always bring us the annunciation of God's designs. As a rule, they are at first incomprehensible to our limited minds, but with time, angelic light helps us see their wisdom.

Quoting the angel's initial greeting, we respond: "Hail Mary, full of grace ..."

> *"Behold the handmaid of the Lord — be it done unto me according to your word."*

This is the answer upon which St. Gabriel and all of heaven — indeed, God himself — was waiting. Mary says "Yes." As the Father had proclaimed "Let there be light!" at the beginning of time, thus creating the blessed spirits, Mary proclaims "let it be done unto me according to your word" in the fullness of time, fulfilling the will of the Father carried by one of those blessed spirits. The angel announces God's plan, but he also awaits our free answer. Without it, the plan will not be realized. God wills our voluntary participation. Though the demands of God may be trying and the immediate logic far from clear, it will only be if we "let it be done according to *his* word" that great things can be conceived. In Mary's case, that great thing was the incarnate Son of God himself.

We respond: "Hail Mary, full of grace . . ."

"And the Word was made flesh and dwelt among us."

This is the fruit of obeying the angel, for obeying his word is obeying God's word. "And the angel departed from her" (Lk. 1:38). St. Gabriel is gone and does not linger to be spotlighted or marveled at. His mission is to glorify God and fulfill his commands. That achieved, he withdraws. But though his visit was short and almost business-like, he left the whole of Christendom quoting his salutation in chorus, as it will continue to do so until the end of time:

"Hail Mary, full of grace!"

We have already seen how the choirs of angels are divided into three great Rings, with one turned exclusively to God in his glory, one embracing the entire physical creation and one turned to the earth and man. Now as we meditate the mystery of Mary and the variety of titles under which she is venerated, we notice that they too follow a certain order.

The most spiritual of all her titles, the most "angelic," one might say, is the Immaculate Conception. The Seraphim, Cherubim and Thrones honor Our Lady especially under this title. The pure spirits, in the very highest regions of their purity, honor the Purest Virgin, conceived without the stain of original sin. Indeed, so sublime is this title, so close to the most remote altitudes of the highest Ring of angels, that the Church secured full certitude regarding this holy truth only after centuries of theological reflection and prayer. Prominent theologians, including St. Thomas Aquinas, had reservations about it, and only in 1854 was it proclaimed dogma. Still, that high angelic title is not the noblest of her salutations.

We look at Mary differently when we salute her with the noblest and highest of all her titles: Mother of God! The Church defined this truth already in AD 431. Under this title, the angels of the third Ring honor Our Lady. Even here, the last shall be first. It was here on earth that she became the Mother of our Redeemer. This is the title that warms our hearts, that fills us with joy and consolation, for it is the motherly office of Mary that meets the deepest and most human needs of our souls.

For the angels, however, Mary's motherhood is less comprehensible than her Immaculate Conception. She is *our* Mother, not the angels'. And it is only the angels of the lower three choirs — the Virtues, Archangels and Angels — who, because of their greater proximity to man, can most readily approach the Blessed Virgin in her maternal role. Many other subsidiary titles are interwoven with this one: Refuge of Sinners, Help of Christians, Comforter of the Afflicted, Cause of our Joy, among others.

There is, however, a third group of titles that have an unmistakably different ring to them, for we speak of Our Lady also as *Queen*. In the Litany of Loreto, the last eleven invocations begin with this regal title. This teaches us that Mary is not only the Immaculate Conception, the Virgin Most Pure, the Inviolate One, the House of Gold (first Ring); and not only the Mother of God and of us all, our Comforter, Refuge and Help (third Ring). Beyond these perfections she is also the majestic and powerful Queen Regent of all creation: Queen of Patriarchs, of Prophets, of Apostles; Queen of all Saints; indeed, Queen Assumed Bodily into Heaven. It is under the complex of these majestic and august titles that the angels of the middle choirs of Dominations, Powers and Princes honor Our Lady. She is not their Mother, but she is most definitely, and for the angels most happily, their supernatural sovereign.

We began with the Genesis prophecy of the woman who would crush the head of the serpent. It was through Our Lady's Immaculate Conception that this pulverization began. It is still very much in progress. Only by uniting ourselves with Our Lady *and* with her millions of holy subjects, the holy angels, can we help her to achieve the victory of her Immaculate Heart. She is the Immaculate Conception with the Seraphim, Cherubim and Thrones in the heaven above the heavens; she is the Queen of the Universe with the Dominations, Powers and Princes over all the vast cosmos; and she is the most holy Mother of God with the Virtues, Archangels and Angels here on our so battle-worn earth. All the angels, in whatever choir, are focusing their attention ever more on this battlefield as the struggles of our times unfold.

In the Apocalypse, Our Lady appears in her full motherly identification with the Church. With all three parts of God's creation, she is portrayed as the Immaculate Mother and Queen, experiencing in apocalyptical fulfillment what was to be "done unto her according to God's word." We read in Apocalypse 12:1:

> And a great sign appeared in heaven, a woman clothed
> with the sun [the glorified human nature redeemed by her
> Son] with the moon under her feet [the material creation],
> and on her head a crown of twelve stars [the holy angels].

In Mary—and in Mary alone—man, cosmos, and angel all find the Mother, the Queen, and the Immaculate Sanctuary God originally planned for them. The serpent had tried to foil the design from top to bottom, but all he managed to do was to occasion a transfiguration of the story into a longer and still more marvelous drama. And at the end of it all, after he makes his last foolhardy attempt to devour the Child that Mary and the Church bring forth (12:4), he will be defeated, and his swollen head forever crushed.

8

The Church's Servants

ACCORDING TO SCRIPTURE, OUR FIRST explicit encounter with the holy angels was after the expulsion from Paradise. At what should have been its welcoming gate, we found ourselves face to face with the Cherubim—their sharp, burning swords pointing our way. The message was clear: we were no longer welcome. Between us and Paradise these august spirits were flourishing the "word of God . . . living and active, sharper than any two-edged sword, piercing to the division of soul and spirit, of joints and marrow, and discerning the thoughts and intentions of the heart" (Hb. 4:12). This should give us pause to reflect upon our relationship to both Paradise and the angels.

The Garden of Eden was planted by God "in the east" (Gn. 2:8). It was to be the place for man to "grow and multiply, and fill the earth, and subdue it" (Gn. 1:28). The symbolic "east" suggests that we were created close to our origin, that is, close to God—theologically put, in the state of grace. Through the ensuing trial of our love, we were to be accepted into the fullness of God's glory, and that meant we were destined not only to stand in his presence, but, far more intimately, to "dwell with him." This abode, however, would have to be freely chosen by submitting to God's will regarding the mysterious Tree of Knowledge. This source of enlightenment could not be forced upon us. We know only too well the outcome of this trial, but let us consider the Garden for a moment. We were driven from its precincts, but — and this is the good part — the rest of sacred history would be the long and eventful narrative of how our relationship to God and his dwelling was to be reconfigured.

The river of grace that flowed "out of Eden to water the Garden" (Gn. 2:10) divided into four rivers.

(It bears reminding that here, early in Genesis — as will also be the case late in the New Testament, in the Apocalypse — we are in the presence of events and realities so primordial, or in the Apocalypse so eschatological, that only symbolic and "mythical" language can venture near them. But unlike most myths and symbols, what are referenced here are very real times and places, and truths as solid — indeed more solid — than those of secular history. They are just too distant and unfamiliar to be described in literal terms.)

Thus, God's first *home* for us was to be a Garden bounded by four symbolic rivers. We still live by preference in four-sided houses and rooms; we still speak of the four directions, the four elements, the four moral virtues, the four temperaments, and so on. God's grace had originally constituted us in a state of perfect order and harmony, symbolized by this Garden of four rivers, supernaturally surrounding and sustaining our natural, quaternal structure.

After having proven our love and obedience by following the divine ordinance regarding the Tree of Knowledge, we would eventually have been admitted to the inner sanctuary of God's glory. We would have joined the highest angels in a life of praise inconceivable to our minds today. But that plan was frustrated, and by the willful interference of our own disobedience. We foolishly chose to try our hand at "understanding" evil by doing it. The performance of evil acts, however, brings darkness, not light. Only a saint can understand sin. As Fulton Sheen once said, there is only one thing on earth you never learn more about through experience, and that is sin.

The infinite God, however, is not easily frustrated. After our fall from grace, he immediately opened the stores of a divine "reserve plan." Thus began the much longer, but to all appearances much more glorious, design of our Redemption and Sanctification. The promise regarding Mary has already been mentioned. We shall now pick up the story where it foreshadows the rebuilding of a created sanctuary where God's majesty can once again dwell. This would be our only hope to finally get past those sharp, Cherubic swords. The sanctuary will evolve through history in stages of progressive blueprints, from the Ark of Noah to the Ark of the Covenant, from the Tabernacle in the desert to the Temple in the city, from what will come to be known as the Church, and then on to its consummate architecture in the New Jerusalem.

When we fell, and the Cherubim stood suddenly and sternly at the gates of our lost home, that home itself seemed to withdraw into the sky. Some mystics claimed to have sighted it on a high mountain. Dante put it in the Southern Hemisphere, still imagined as a highland of sun and treasure to the medieval mind. It will be more theologically coherent if we simply picture it as withdrawing into the choirs of the angels, far above the reach of all our towers of Babel (Gn. 11). The earth is too fragile for glory quite yet. After all, we were left "to till the ground from which we were taken" (Gn. 3:23), that is, to labor in the state of gross material nature, and a wounded nature at that.

High in the choirs of angels, the former Garden of Paradise is being repurposed into the future City of God. One day it will descend upon the earth as the final dwelling place of God with his creation. Much of the language used is of course figurative. The "descent" of the City may simply refer to the progressive sanctification and transformation of the world as we know it. Cosmic annihilation, at any rate, does not figure in God's plans. The cosmos will be changed, but certainly not destroyed.

"For the creation waits with eager longing for the revealing of the sons of God; for the creation was subjected to futility, not of its own will but by the will of him who subjected it in hope; because the creation itself will be set free from its bondage to decay and obtain the glorious liberty of the children of God. We know that the whole creation has been groaning with labor pains together until now" (Rm. 8:19–22).

We read about that final consummation at the very end of the last book of the Bible: "Behold, I make all things new" (Apoc. 21:5); and "Behold, the dwelling of God is with men" (Apoc. 23:3). That celestial metropolis, full of angelic occupants, is glimpsed at times by the prophets of the Old Covenant under other figures, such as the "Chariot of God" (cf. Ezek. 1). But long before it begins its symbolic descent, "coming *down* out of heaven from God" (Apoc. 21:2), we, in the meantime, are being primed for our new habitat. By following instructions on building small dwellings on earth — as if in miniature imitation of that celestial abode — we begin to relearn what it means to dwell with God.

With the building of Noah's ark (Gn. 6), a dimly perceived historical fact rises before our eyes, still nestled in the symbolic ambience of the first eleven chapters of Genesis. Here is the first post-paradisiacal dwelling place for God's children. But it is still, like the primordial chaos (Gn. 1:1–2), "moving over the face of the waters." Only with Abraham (Gn. 12ff.) does the promise of solid land give assurance that the divine dwelling will indeed regain foothold in creation.

Later on, God will say to Moses: "Make me a sanctuary, that I may dwell in your midst" (Ex. 25:8). And on Mount Sinai, Moses is shown the archetypal dwelling in heaven that is to be the model for the tabernacle on earth. "And you shall erect the tabernacle according to the plan for it which has been shown you on the mountain" (Ex. 26:30). Accordingly, instead of the four rivers, we have the four sides of the tabernacle; later, with Solomon, the four-sided Temple of Sion will become the great Old Testament mock-up of God's future dwelling among men. The whole of the Old Testament Covenant revolves around this evolving divine edifice and the cult God ordains to be performed within it. From the Temple cult to the Christian liturgy of today, we are being trained to assume again the position of love and obedience we lost in Paradise.

Through its infidelity to the Law and pursuit of false gods, the Chosen People will largely be unable to recognize Christ as Emmanuel, God-with-us. They will look on as he and his body are destroyed just as the Roman Emperor was to destroy the actual Temple of Jerusalem in the year 70. But before Our Lord entered the Passion and submitted to this death, he had taken his Apostles into the four-walled room of the Cenacle and instituted the Sacrifice of the New Covenant in his Blood. That first Christian assembly became the model for all the churches to come, and the true successor of the Temple of Jerusalem.

Here, through the Eucharist, God was to be present in an altogether new way. By now entering the temple of the human body — with its four humors, four temperaments, four limbs and a soul destined to initial perfection in the four moral virtues — the final preparations are being made. His mysteriously glorified body was now to be made present in the new "showbread" of the Christian liturgy (Ex. 25:30). The construction of his new headquarters among us, and indeed in us, is now fully underway.

The Church and its greatest treasure, the Holy Eucharist, continue and perfect the work of the Tabernacle in the desert and the Temple in Sion. All these were new terrestrial dwelling places for the God who had been banished from his own creation by sin. But the Eucharist, which *is* Christ himself, is the definitive building block for his final and Apocalyptical dwelling in the renewed creation.

Cherubim stood with their "flaming swords which turned every way" at the gates of Paradise. Cherubim were also carved at the two sides of the Mercy-Seat in the Temple, where God spoke to man (Ex. 25:18–21). The Mass too begins with the sword of Scripture and doctrine, in which God speaks to man in the Liturgy of the Word. But now the august word is buffered, as it were, by the humanity of Christ, and we pass unharmed through the sword's edge of those holy utterances, and on into the intimacy of the sanctuary. And in the Eucharistic Preface, we turn with confidence to the angels — "with angels and archangels" — as we proceed to the Consecration.

Likewise, before the Church inherits the full perfection of the New Jerusalem, she too will have to turn to the angels in the mysteries of the Apocalypse. And that means experiencing the fulfilment of Our Lord's promise that "he will send out the angels, and gather the elect from the four winds, from the ends of the earth to the ends of heaven" (Mk. 13:26). And as for the purification, he insists that it is *the angels* who will perform these last works of his Church's cleansing; it is they who will "gather out of his Kingdom all causes of sin and all evildoers" (Mt. 13:41).

The entire book of the Apocalypse can be seen as a working out of the Paschal Mystery of Christ's suffering, death and resurrection on the global level. Ever again, in its history, the whole Church will suffer the fury of hell, at times apparently die, and then, suddenly, rise from the dead just as dramatically as did Jesus on Easter Morning. But one day it will be his whole Mystical Body that rises:

> Then I saw a new heaven and a new earth; for the first heaven and the first earth had passed away, and the sea was no more. And I saw the holy city, New Jerusalem, coming down out of heaven from God, prepared as a bride adorned for her husband; and I heard a loud voice from the throne saying, "Behold, the dwelling of God is with men".... And he who sat upon the throne said, "Behold, I make all things new." (Apoc. 21:1–3, 5)

It becomes evident that angel and man, and with them the material cosmos, all have parts to play in the new order of creation. Significantly, we are told in the Apocalypse that the very measures of the Heavenly City's walls are *"a man's measure, that is, an angel's"* (Apoc. 21:17). But if the measure has become the same, either humans will have become more angelic, or angels more human — or *both.* At the end of time, man and angel will have realized the full measure of their common praise of Christ, as their voices join with the cosmic music of material creation in the worship of the Triune God.

9

Our Guardians

WE HAVE SPENT MUCH TIME IN THESE pages considering the large context of the angels' role in creation, their Rings and Choirs, the great events of the dawn of history and the future enormities and promises of the Apocalypse. One might feel a bit lost in all this splendor and magnitude. What about my own spiritual life? What have the angels to do with the everyday affairs I spend most of my time with? To this we must finally turn.

Christ is the one Lord of all creation—human, angelic and material. To his Church and its work in preparing God's definitive dwelling place all creation looks, including the highest Seraphim. Furthermore, among all the glories of Mary and all the "angelic" privileges with which God has vested her, no honor is so high as that of being Mother of God. This title, too, was granted to her on earth. The entire drama of creation revolves now around the story of man. The fallen angels can win consolation prizes, as it were, but only when we consent to sin. The holy angels, in turn, can experience supplemental increases in their beatitude through the sanctification of man. "There is joy before the angels of God over one sinner who repents" (Lk. 15:10). The whole heavy gate of history now swings on the weak, squeaky hinges of the human will.

Because of all this, one final truth about the holy angels is of the highest importance. We run the risk of thinking of it as peripheral, supplementary—indeed, "a nice touch," as it were, but hardly anything that plays an integral role in our sanctification. But we are wrong. I am referring, of course, to the teaching about our guardian angels. If the relationship of man to angel in the future life is as intimate as Scripture suggests, the bond of guardianship that unites man and angel in this life must be full of mysteries waiting to be unlocked.

St. Paul gives us a clue in the letter to the Ephesians as to what these mysteries might be. Speaking about the Gospel and the Paschal Mystery, which is its very heart, he celebrates the "unsearchable riches of Christ." He regards it as his job to "make all men see what is the plan of the mystery hidden for ages in God who created all things; that *through the Church* the manifold wisdom of God *might now be made known to the Principalities and Powers in the heavenly places*" (emphasis added). What can this mean? It seems to suggest that the angels too are in store for a revelation. Perhaps the meaning is quite simply this: it will be through the Church—that is, through us as members of Christ—that the angels shall be escorted into the fullness of the mystery of Christ.

Why would this be necessary? The answer should be obvious. Of themselves, the angels do not have a natural experience of what it is to be human. But the mystery of our salvation, in the service of which they stand, was worked out in the Sacred Humanity of Our Lord, and indeed, through very human suffering. And even beyond this, through the experience completely unknown to an angel: the experience of death. If Christ is truly the Lord of *all* creation, and both man *and* angel will share in his glory in eternity, a question presents itself. Has God provided no means at all for the angel to come closer to the *human* mystery of Jesus? In God's infinite goodness, is the angel to be forever denied the grace of looking into the things "into which angels long to look" (1 Pet. 1:12)?

Let us suppose it is true that the angels are assigned to individual human beings for the length of their lives, to guard and enlighten them, serving as conduits of countless actual graces. It would likewise be true that they would be forbidden to force us or in any way infringe on our freedom of will. This brings something to mind. Would this not be a trying task for an angel? To be sure, it is the beatitude of the angel to fulfill God's will wherever and however he ordains. But does that mean it is easy? Christ came to save us out of his love for us, embracing human suffering as a means of that salvation. But could anything be further from the truth than to suggest that it was easy?

The Franciscan theologian Duns Scotus speculated that guardian angels may be taken from any of the nine choirs of angels. It seems that their role is one of such importance — not only for man but *also* for the angel — that God may have willed that all angels share in this grace. It is commonly accepted, however, that the guardian angels are from the lowest choir, the ninth, or at least from the lower choirs. Otherwise, the angels would be too far beyond human nature to be able to empathize with us. But perhaps God allows higher angels to serve for a time in the lower choir, and in this way to imitate Christ, who "for a little while was made lower than the angels" (Hb. 2:9). This could be the angels' emulation of their Lord's Foot Washing — a sort of "prince and pauper" exchange for the high nobility among the pure spirits.

Christ, "though he was in the form of God, did not count equality with God a thing to be grasped, but emptied himself, taking the form of a servant, being born in the likeness of men. And being found in human form he humbled himself and became obedient unto death, even death on a Cross" (Phil. 2:6–8). The angel longs to follow Christ. He cannot suffer and die like a man, but one thing he can do: he can "empty himself" of the expression of his angelic glory and power, "take the form of a servant" by humbly ministering to the needs of a poor and weak human being, and thus practice a humility and obedience which, in small measure, is comparable to that by which Our Lord saved the world.

Thus, the work of guardian angels, constantly taught by the Church (*Roman Catechism*, IV, and in the new *Catechism*, n. 336) and testified to in Scripture (Mt. 18:10; Acts 12:15; the entire book of Tobit), turns out to be a grace both for man and for angel. For the angel, being placed, in the words of St. Basil, "at [man's] side as educator and guide, directing his life," the opportunity is given to come closer to the reality of the Incarnation. But conversely, for man, it is a chance to become more attuned to the most sublime, the most "angelic," of the great, central truths of the faith: that God is Father, Son, and Holy Spirit.

By practicing the renunciation necessarily involved in his demanding task, the angel too can come to share more deeply in the "unsearchable riches of Christ." The Holy Trinity and the Incarnation are the two basic dogmas of the faith; angel and man are like mutual tutors in these two complementary mysteries, each one illuminating the other.

But there is more. The third great mystery of the faith is that of the Most Holy Eucharist. Here we find ourselves back at our opening reflections on God's threefold creation. For if the Holy Trinity is the highest spiritual mystery, deeply akin to the world of the angels; and the Incarnation the mystery most deeply immersed in the world of man; the mystery of the Eucharist would be the one that touches in an altogether new way the physical universe, which complements the angelic and the human as the third division of God's threefold creation. On the night before he suffered, Our Lord reached down into the depths of the material cosmos, lifting up the humble material elements of bread and wine by transforming them into the mystery of his Body and Blood.

Together with our guardian angels, we *both* kneel in profound adoration before this third mystery. Under the appearances of bread, a product of the material creation ordered entirely to the livelihood of our body, God receives the adoration of both of his other creatures. St. Paul teaches us that "the creation itself will be set free from its bondage to decay and obtain the glorious liberty of the children of God.... The whole creation has been groaning in travail together until now" (Rm. 8:21–22). Through the Holy Eucharist, this final liberation of the physical universe from the "Prince of this World" (Jn. 12:31) begins, and the "transformation of the world" through the "new commandment of love" (*Gaudium*

74

et Spes, n. 40) opens the first passageways to the New Jerusalem.

St. Margaret Mary Alacoque, to whom the mysteries of Christ's Sacred Heart were revealed, also received graced insights into the relationship of man and angel to the Eucharist. During adoration of the Sacrament, the angels told her they had come:

> to associate themselves with her to render to him a continual homage of love, adoration, and praise; and that for this, they would take her place before the Holy Sacrament in order that through their mediation she could love without interruption, and that, in the same way, they could participate in her love, suffering in her person as she rejoiced in theirs. (*Autobiography*, paragraph 101)

Through the angels, we increase in loving adoration of the Trinitarian God; through us, the angels approach the Paschal Mystery of Christ into which they long to look. But nowhere do these complementary ministries interpenetrate more and bring forth more intimate and lasting fruit than at the moment of Holy Communion.

CONCLUSION

DESPITE ALL THAT WE HAVE SEEN IN OUR treatment of the angels, one might still have the uneasy feeling that the angels are just too much for us, and better left alone—or at least postponed for the afterlife. After all, does not Scripture admonish us: "Seek not the things that are too high for you, and search not into things above your ability" (Sir. 3:21)? And it is so easy to develop an unhealthy curiosity about such things. Is it not sufficient for us to adhere to Christ, venerate his Mother, follow the directives of his Church and "work out our salvation in fear and trembling" (Phil. 2:12)?

Perhaps this was sufficient in earlier times, but things have taken on an urgency today. To be sure, not everyone is called to be an angel expert, and to dwell long and deeply on these truths. But without the angels, the Christian and Biblical vision of reality lacks an integral dimension of its total worldview. One should also read further in the famous passage from Sirach quoted above, for the following line reads: "But the things that God has commanded you, think on them always" (Sir. 3:22).

That is to say, we should not pry into matters God has hidden from us, such as the hour and day of the end of the world (Acts 1:7). But things that he *has* revealed to us (and many things about the angels *have* been revealed), and things he has commanded us ("Give heed to him [the angel] and hearken to his voice, do not rebel against him . . . for my Name is in him" [Ex. 23:20]) — on these things we must think, and always.

Pope St. John Paul II has urged that the teaching about the angels is "a truth which must be profoundly important for every Christian" ("Catechesis on the Angels," 1986, part 6 no. 5). We must not become obsessed with them, but we are obliged to be aware of them. The current battle within and outside the Church cannot be properly understood unless we integrate an understanding of the angels into our faith.

As Vatican II's *Pastoral Constitution on the Church in the Modern World* has taught: "The whole of man's history has been the story of our combat with the powers of evil, stretching, so our Lord tells us, from the very dawn of history until the last day. Finding himself in the midst of the battlefield man has to struggle to do what is right" (*Gaudium et Spes*, n. 37).

In that struggle, as Pope John Paul asserts, "we are powerfully helped by the good angels." We must turn to them, and we must invite them. Their hands are bound and their power throttled, as long as we ignore them. But when they are invited and allowed to work in us and through us, they can unfold their many-sided ministries within the Church and powerfully help us to secure the victory of Christ.

The book of the Apocalypse is full of angels. So are the times before us. Let us take to heart the last words spoken by the "Angelic Pastor," Venerable Pius XII, to a group of Americans five days before his death; for he spoke to them about the angels:

"You will spend, God grant it, an eternity of joy with them; BEGIN TO KNOW THEM NOW."

PART 2
Angels That Fall

"Lucifer" by Gustave Doré

INTRODUCTION

G.K. CHESTERTON ONCE ENJOINED ALL followers of Christ to take fallen angels seriously, but not in order to alarm or unsettle us, but surprisingly just the opposite: "The Christian way is to believe there is a positive evil somewhere and fight it; for then everything else will be really jolly and pleasant.... Roses will be twice as red if you believe in the Devil. Skies will be twice as blue if you believe in the Devil."

It is with this alert but buoyant disposition that we must embark upon the disagreeable topic of the second part of our book — not with an attitude of flippancy, but neither with one of morbid curiosity. In fact, let us not be hypocritical: we already know all too well what is under discussion.

We are aware of the weakness and malice that can flourish within our own breasts. But beyond this, we frequently sense that over and above (or should I say beneath and below?) the evil produced by our human misdeeds, a further strange and subversive force is up to no good in this world. It is a fact difficult to dodge. Many of those who deny it have simply yet to come face to face with an utterly wicked act, or, more likely, are among the masters of the modern art of sustained distraction, and thus keep the experience in comfortably low profile. And of course, some few deny it for the simple reason that they are part of it, and denying it is one of their duties.

As for Christians, however, the Faith leaves us little choice: we must take this strange world of darkness seriously. But seriously does not mean solemnly. Identifying and isolating the mechanism of disease is the first step toward rejoicing in the vigors of health. Likewise, when we are sometimes teased by visions of existential absurdity, it can be strangely comforting to discover that there is an infernal method in the madness of the world. It actually relieves the mind to discover a reason for the wrongness of things, even if the reason can be rather creepy.

Unlike the strained optimisms of the world, the great Christian joys sung by the martyrs and saints are inextricably bound up with their belief in this most vexing of Christian truths: the existence of immaterial agents bent on evil. I will go so far as to say that in this pilgrimage we are on, no truth can fully shine, where this truth is allowed to pale.

And I do mean truth. It matters little whether we like the truth or not. The world not being of our own making, neither are its truths tailored to our finite tastes. But simply by opening our eyes upon the risky battlefield we set our feet on every day, and by seeing that we have been supplied with all sorts of otherworldly weaponry, we really should have one thing straight by now: there is war on earth. We may be commanded to love our enemies, but this does not make them our friends.

Our goal in these reflections will not be to gasp and shudder at horror stories about demonic possession or Satanic atrocities, but rather to simply see the fallen spirits as what they in truth are: defeated creatures, to be sure, but still pitifully bent on stealing the show from God.

What's more, some knowledge of these things is a capital antidote to sloth. And, as Chesterton suggested, there is an unexpected consolation as well: a sense of gusto. You will be surprised at the difference a Christian spirit of combat makes in your ability to live in a world with such a maddening mixture of nobility and depravity. Some may continue to claim that pacifism is a valid political option, but it will never be a valid spiritual option, certainly not for followers of Christ. Our seventh day of rest comes only after six days of struggle. The contest, however, can be invigorating.

There is something in us that likes to fight for a noble cause and go to bed at night knowing that we have struck down some evil and promoted some good. It peppers up our drab existence to know we are engaged in an honorable battle. To quote Chesterton once again:

> This life of ours is a very enjoyable fight, but a very miserable truce. This world can be made beautiful again by beholding it as a battlefield. When we have defined and isolated the evil thing, the colors come back into everything else. When evil things have become evil, good things, in a blazing apocalypse, become good. There are some men who are dreary because they do not believe in God; but there are many others who are dreary because they do not believe in the Devil. (*Charles Dickens*, 205–6)

I

Enemy Number One

W E SHALL BEGIN OUR CONSIDER-
ation of evil agents by going to the very top of the
pyramid of wickedness. What will it help us to identify dozens of enemies if we have failed first to properly size up

83

the worst and most abominable adversary of them all? This will be far from pleasant, and I am afraid profoundly shocking for many a reader, but we must proceed. Only cowardice will make someone flip nervously over the next few pages and pick up the story at chapter 2.

This first fiend is actually a quite diminutive creature, and a very slippery one at that. Nonetheless, he sports a power over my soul and yours that is simply terrifying. He is almost continuously successful in riveting our attention, and whenever his horrible name is even lightly whispered, he is there in a flash. Once we give him our ear, we are soon eating out of his hand, and his grinning face begins to loom over our lives like a cruel slave master. *No army of exorcizing priests has ever succeeded in banishing this one.*

More radical weapons are needed. And what is more, according to moral theology, this little monster is the only one who can actually steal our eternal beatitude. All the infernal legions of Satan cannot get even close to our soul unless he first gives the signal. He reigns supreme in our smug and tiny universe and is, without possible competition, Enemy Number One.

I shall now reveal his name. We do not know too many demonic names from the pages of Scripture, but this one is available in the pages of any book. It is smeared all over the newspapers; it is emblazoned across movie screens and chanted on TV; it is on the lips of every man and woman on earth. This is unfortunate, for we know that carelessly mentioning the names of fallen spirits can have the effect of invoking them. But enough of this; you must know by now who I am talking about. In English, his name is "me," although the psychologists have taught us to use the Latin pronoun, "ego."

We will save ourselves a world of deceptions if we get this straight. So, read carefully: our own weak, potentially perverse and easily misguided ego is by far the most dangerous "fallen spirit" around. Real demons can do nothing of permanent harm to our souls if our own free will does not first give in to sin. The very notion of hell only possesses theological cogency insofar as each one of us is perfectly capable of making it real. Just like a stubborn little brat, I can go on telling God "No, no, no . . ." for as long as I want, even, theoretically, forever. Paradoxically, there is no more striking proof of the reality of our created freedom than precisely this capacity. Theologians, however, will qualify this by pointing out that "freedom" to sin is actually just a sign of our free will, but not actually a full exercise thereof. We can be truly free only when we choose God.

Still, no one can make me change my mind, if "ego" doesn't want to change it. Ignorance of this fact and underestimation of the peril that dwells in our own breasts will only make any study of demonology a dangerous endeavor. If you, dear reader, are unconvinced by this, please put the book down. You would be better off knowing nothing more about the fallen angels, if you refuse to know more about your fallen ego. Although few of us are possessed by demons, I suspect most all of us are regularly possessed by our egos.

Let us recall when Christ was once preparing to cast out a legion of demons (of the Gerasene demoniac, reported in all three Synoptic Gospels), and they first asked him if, pretty please, they could be banished to a hoard of swine scavenging about in the area? Remember how Our Lord obliged, but how it killed the poor pigs? Well, as long as we keep to our swinish, egocentric ways, we will hardly be better off than those pigs.

The readers who have read this far must be ready by now for their first exorcism. So, let us begin. My first question to your ego is: When did you last examine your conscience and ask God's pardon for your sins? Catholics can go to confession, but everyone can repent, and should. Getting Enemy Number One under some kind of control is our first duty before reading part two of the present book.

By humbly submitting ourselves to spiritual purification, calling our sins by their names so that we might profit from the graces of healing shame, we soon will be on the road to restored innocence. Should there be any fallen angels in the vicinity, we can rest assured they will feel unwelcome around souls full of humility, praise and love (and other horrible things), and scout around instead for the nearest pigsty.

2

Do You Believe in Rattlesnakes?

CHARLES BAUDELAIRE, THE FRENCH SYM-
bolist poet of the 19th century, is credited with the oft-
quoted remark that "the Devil's cleverest wile is to convince us that he does not exist." This observation might ring a bit
hollow today, for, unlike Baudelaire, we have the blood-soaked
20th century in our recent past. The face of evil has mutated so
dramatically in our times that Christians often find themselves
grappling with more bizarre affronts to orthodoxy than those of
mere disbelief. But even today, many try to make sense of horrific
moral evil by attributing it to human agency alone, or perhaps to
mental illness.

It is true that our own souls are quite competent in the production of our very own sins of weakness and malice. But although
there may not be "a devil behind every tree," we still might find
one or two behind *some* trees. When learning about crimes of
horrific cruelty, we find ourselves asking how a human being could
possibly do such a thing.

Even when we commit our own wicked deeds, in the aftermath
we may exclaim: "What got into me?" What (or who) indeed! In
order to understand our possibilities for both good and evil, we
must recognize that we possess two interfaces with two realms

of other persons: our corporeal interface through which we see and communicate with other human beings outside of us, and our spiritual interface, by which we engage with our own ideas and also with the spiritual world that is both beyond us and within us. We get input from both sources. The title of this book refers to this second world of persons.

Against the evidence, many continue to impugn traditional belief that there are also supernatural sources of evil. Baudelaire would say they still have not learned that promoting such disbelief is one of the oldest and most successful strategies of the Devil. When you doubt that he is there, he is much freer to move about as he pleases.

Beyond this old-fashioned disbelief, there are two other principal attitudes one can assume regarding demons. One is a far stranger position which has regained currency only recently, although ultimately harking back at least to the high noon of occultism in the European Renaissance. It turns out to be of a rather spooky nature. This approach concedes that what we call the demons do indeed exist, only adding that they are not as dreadful as tradition has unkindly maintained. Since the third position is the view of demonic reality taken by traditional Christianity, and the one we are defending for the rest of this book, we shall pause briefly on this second, rather bizarre variety.

It has to be said that there is much to be preferred in the first, time-honored position. The honorable old atheists of the past, the ones who quoted Voltaire and Bertrand Russell (or today maybe Richard Dawkins or Stephen Fry), will point with a snicker at all our pictures of red devils and slithering serpents. But they at least have their reasons. According to them, modern man is riding on the wave of an eventual scientific explanation for absolutely everything. They feel assured that the devils will soon be definitively explained away, as has almost everything else once called "supernatural." These materialists are often pompous and annoying, but their very secularism shields them from far more vicious sorts of pride than this. They think the world is all that exists, so at least they cannot pride themselves on being unworldly. Laying all their hopes in scientific knowledge, they at least try to measure their convictions by something outside of themselves.

But attempting to understand the second type of debunker is a much frostier intellectual exercise. On this view, the Devil does not exist as an evil being, but rather as a power in the universe, or perhaps in human nature itself. But it is a power with which we have not yet properly come to terms. More recently we have been trained by modern cinema to see the "Force" as having both a good and an evil side. The story goes that we have been afraid of this negative power for millennia, repressing its manifold invitations into the murky depths of our unconscious and giving it hundreds of horrifying names. Its operations have been projected all over the sky of ancient mythology, deep into the nightmares of Greek tragedy, and up and down the moralists' lists of forbidden sins.

The "Devil," they say, is just a dimension of existence which only fully realized humans are valiant and brave enough to acknowledge as their own. Throughout history, isolated individuals have taken this power into their hands, but only to be chided by the still puerile society in which they lived; often enough, they were persecuted as sorcerers or burned as witches. Only now, they say, as we progress into our enlightened 21st century, has mankind finally grown up. We may at long last lay our human hands upon secrets of knowledge and power before which earlier generations shuddered in trepidation.

Some members of the so-called New Age Movement take this view, as do, of course, those who directly engage in occultism. To them, the so-called "forces of evil" are only potentialities in the cosmos or in our own psyche, and for most of them, do not finally constitute actual spiritual beings in themselves. Our forebears gave these potentialities mythological names or attempted to bring them together into various categories of esoteric knowledge. In this way, they may have even been given a measure of meaning in our development. But finally, they are just parts of us or of the world around us, or possibly just components of the accumulated deposit of human experience. Like fire or wild horses, they just need to be domesticated.

Some occultists may even agree with the traditional Christian position that they are not mere products of human imagination or neurosis, but real beings of some sort. But they will go on to say that man's misunderstanding of these occult entities has been in large part due to the slanderous misdeeds of the Christian tradition. The time has come, they inform us, to realize that the so-called "fallen" angels are just spiritual agencies whose message has been garbled by human stupidity and fear, and who long to share with us their many-splendored gifts.

Although of recent popularity in contemporary culture, this sort of thing is hardly new. Aside from some few deliberately malicious and depraved agents, almost all the practitioners of the occult arts believe that what they deal in are basically good and beneficent influences. They will protest that they, and the forces they trade in, have just been misunderstood. Unjustly maligned by the ignorant masses, or by jealous religious prelates, all they claim to be offering is initiation into the higher secrets of the universe. What is new in our times is that this generous offer has, for the first time in Christian history, been graciously accepted by tens of thousands of fallen-away believers.

To Chesterton is attributed the remark that the problem with ceasing to believe in God is not that you thereafter believe in nothing, but that you believe in *anything*. We see this on display in the plethora of cults and "spiritualities" that have arisen in recent times.

Still, by and large, most of the opposition to a Christian-based demonology will come from the doubters. Those, however, who persist in this disbelief may as well disbelieve in rattlesnakes, black widow spiders and scorpions. It does bring transitory comfort to pretend they are not there — at least, until the bite. As Pope St. Paul VI insisted in his November 15, 1972, address:

> We know that this dark and destructive being really exists and is still active; he is the sophistical perverter of man's moral equipoise, the malicious seducer who knows how to penetrate us.... It would be very important to return to a study of Catholic teaching on the Devil and the influence he is able to wield, but nowadays little attention is paid to it. (*Deliver Us From Evil*, "Il Nemico Occulto Che Semina Errori")

Fifteen years later, his successor felt moved to make the point with even greater emphasis:

The evil that exists, the disorder that lives in society, the incoherence of man, the interior breakdown of which mankind is victim is not only the result of original sin, but also the effects of the dark and nefarious actions of Satan, that destroyer of the moral equilibrium of humanity, whom St. Paul did not hesitate to call "the god of this world" (2 Cor. 4:3). (Address at Monte Gargano, 1987, n. 3)

For the rest of these pages, we will try to give to this teaching the attention the recent popes have called for. And we shall begin by asking how such a thing as a devil came to exist in the first place. The problem should bother any thinking person. At first glance, the existence of fallen creatures seems to suggest that God was somehow remiss in the business of creating his universe. If it was known that this was going to be one of the outcomes of his creation (and how could the All-Knowing not know it?), why were the plans not changed or adjusted? As usual, however, our first glance is acutely myopic.

Only when we understand what the "falling" was about to begin with will we see that divine plans for creation are filled with a wisdom above and beyond the conundrums that perplex our created minds. Certainly, the Creator could have played it "safer" and resolved not to call us to such dangerous heights as he did. But one thing is clear: in that safer world, his love for us would also have been a safer and tamer love. We can be sure that there is not an angel or a saint in heaven who would not insist that this wilder love was well worth the risk.

3

On the Falling of Angels

AFTER THE SEVENTY-TWO DISCIPLES HAD been sent out by Our Lord on their first mini-mission, "as lambs in the midst of wolves," they returned bubbling over with enthusiasm, and began at once to tell the Master of their apostolic adventures. As a kind of climax to their excited report, St. Luke records them as exclaiming: "Lord, even the demons are subject to us in your Name!" At those words, something deep in Jesus must have stirred, for as had happened so often before, an innocent comment drew forth a solemn and haunting declaration from the mouth of the God-Man: "I saw Satan like lightning falling from heaven" (Lk. 10:18).

Jesus does not say that he saw the fall of Satan, but rather the *falling* of Satan. This invites us to embark upon the rather difficult and somewhat vexing topic of just what a falling angel could possibly be.

Our High Vocation

Most of us have had the strange double experience of being attracted to some high vantage point to enjoy a view and then being scared out of our socks as we looked down over the edge. Maybe it was a mountain ridge, or just a tall building. In either case, it was exciting to climb to the top, whether by rope or by elevator, and the view was indeed breathtaking. But a bit too much breath was taken as we looked back down from the heights, and our knees began knocking beneath us. And why? Obviously because we were overcome by the fear of falling. This common experience is a natural reflection in our human bodies of a very supernatural condition in the make-up of our human souls.

Our Creator's plan for his creation was for something far more adventurous than a video game. He made us truly and dangerously free. He gave his angels and human beings the formidable capacity to respond by a free choice to his divine invitation. But invitation to what? This is where the dizzying heights come into the picture. God invited all his free creatures to choose a direct share in his infinite and eternal life, beyond every created dream and out of the reach of any concept a created mind could generate. But it would be ours for the having — providing, of course, we choose to have it. And the most puzzling part of it all is that we may choose not to. We are free to settle for less. But here already our knees begin to knock, for the *less* we settle for is not a compromise, but something more like an abyss.

People today are hard put to appreciate the stakes of Christian existence. We subconsciously suspect that there can be some kind of compromise between Christ and Satan, a sort of détente between supernatural superpowers. After all, if only we avoid felonies, is it not enough to just be nice to each other, without chasing after some inflated idea of "beatitude"? "Almighty God is hardly going to waste a nice creature like me," one might think. Thus, we cruise half-consciously through life until a personal tragedy finally breaks the spell.

As the 20th century recedes into the past, perhaps we should be grateful that the Enemy has begun showing his face more openly. Aside from the occultists, most of us have grown so jaded in the face of any serious supernatural prospect as to greet the real thing, whether infernal or heavenly, with neither belief nor disbelief, but rather with a yawn. It could well be that we needed Hitler, Stalin, Mao, Pol Pot, the movie *The Exorcist* or even Charlie Manson, just to get our attention.

The point is this: mediocrity is not an option. God has called us to the heights. For reasons of his own, he has left no middle region of blissful neutrality, but demanded that we either embrace him whole or refuse him whole. Of course, there is a more and less in beatitude, as in the well-known comparison of the full thimble and the full Lake Michigan — equally full, but unequal in capacity. The point is that however "much" our sanctity grows, it must fill us *completely*. In heaven, it is inconceivable that words like "ok" and "all right" or "whatever" might pass the lips of those who know beatitude.

We human beings have our entire life on earth as a proving ground for our wills. The angels, on the other hand, had to make their once and for all decision at the very beginning of the universe. Due to their pure spiritual nature, it could not have been otherwise. The angel saw at once all the consequences of his choice, and thus fixed his will in an irrevocable way on the option he preferred. The angel made this leap once and for all, and his will was thereby fixed for ever in what he wanted for ever. What God ultimately "does" with these resolute refusers — and indeed what he does with any unrepentant creature — lies in his mysterious Providence. Nonetheless, from our human, theological point of view, it does not look good.

How Low Can an Angel Get?

There has been no dearth of wishful thinking and sentimentalism suggesting that the alleged perpetuity of hell is not in keeping with God's boundless mercy. But that is not really the point. An unending hell is not presented as a possibility because God decided on that as the best way to avenge himself on his truant creatures. The whole point is that *they* decided on it. God just gave them freedom, and that gift — like all good things — can be both used and abused. All the mercy an infinite God can muster could not change the fate of a creature which, endowed with a sovereign free will, refused to repent. It would be as impossible as slaking someone's thirst with gallons of water poured over their hands, when they resolutely refused to cup them. The water would simply splash to the ground, as God's words of mercy would echo in the void.

Theologians have always had their work cut out for them when they tried to explain the notion of damnation. Let us put the essential matter as briefly as possible. Man and angel were created with a capacity to receive the gift of God's grace. It was a capacity which only God could activate. We could not deploy it ourselves. We learn that God gave that gift at the very moment of our creation; and we, through sin, forfeited it. Through God's paternal forgiveness, it has been offered to us again in the Redemption.

The point is that although we cannot reach for grace on our own, we can at least sense a longing for something without which we will never be fully happy. Our heart is restless until it rests in God, said St. Augustine. Our faith teaches that every human being, at some time, even if it only be at the moment of his death, is offered the gift of Christ's Redemption. One may say yes, or one may say no. But if it is no, it will only be because the will has been fixed on some good other than God. And that is all it wants. If that fixation of a human will in a creature — be that the creature itself, or sex, or food or power — were to endure unto the very separation of body and soul at death, the human decision of will could become as irrevocable as that of an angel.

What then is hell? It is the possible fixation of a created will (angelic or human) on a good which cannot possibly fill and beatify it. As a result, despite all efforts at self-deception, the poor will is miserable. This is not easy to grasp, but C. S. Lewis dramatized the situation quite effectively in his book *The Great Divorce*. His idea is that if perdition is to make any sense at all, it must be a prison in which the doors have all been locked from the inside, and not from without.

Holy Scripture does teach that "God did not spare the angels when they sinned, but cast them into hell and committed them to pits of nether gloom to be kept until the judgment" (2 Pet. 2:4). But this passage must be read in harmony with another passage from the New Testament, from the letter of Jude: "The angels that did not keep their own position but left their proper dwelling have been kept by him in eternal chains in the nether gloom until the judgment of the great day" (v. 6). God cast them into hell only in the sense that he demanded a yes or no to his divine will and denied his glory to those who said no. If anyone turns away from the gates of heaven, it will be on their own accord. It is inaccurate to imagine them all kicking and screaming to get out. The phrase "until the judgment," however, allows us to hope that God's judgment may have means of moving even the most unrepentant in the end.

Why Such a Falling Out?

When we say the angels had to say yes or no to God's will, what exactly was God's will? Theologians have speculated for centuries on the subject of the trial of the angels. All are more or less agreed that those who fell, fell through pride; but what was it that tried their pride so severely? As we have pointed out in earlier chapters of this book, the 17th-century Jesuit Francisco Suárez argues that in view of the central plan of the Incarnation and the supreme dignity to be accorded to the human nature in Jesus Christ, the trial of the angels' humility may well have involved their willingness (or not) to worship God in the lowly human form.

St. Paul speaks of "the purpose set forth in Christ as a plan for the fullness of time, to unite all things in him, things in heaven and things on earth" (Eph. 1:9–10). He also teaches that "at the name of Jesus every knee should bow, in heaven and on earth and under the earth, and every tongue confess that Jesus Christ is Lord, to the glory of God the Father" (Phil. 2:10–11). So, paradoxically, the dizzying heights to which God was calling all his creatures was in fact a participation in his own unfathomable plunge into deepest humiliation. "Though he was in the form of God, Christ Jesus did not count equality with God a thing to be grasped, but emptied himself, taking the form of a servant, being born in the likeness of men. And being found in human form he humbled himself and became obedient unto death, even death on a cross" (Phil. 2:5–8).

Picking up once again our image of the falling angels hoping to turn the creation upside down, Suárez's idea gives a remarkable new twist to the story. For now it is God himself who is seen to be turning the universe topsy-turvy. And it is the demons who appear to be pleading for a more reasonable arrangement; that is, they would have no problem in keeping God at the top, as long as they would be in second place: angel, then man, and finally the cosmos. The very Creator seemed to be upsetting the whole logic of hierarchy by uniting himself with a mere human, lifting that fleshly creature far above the pure spirits of heaven.

Now we need to make a precision. When the angels fell—that is, when they refused the humbling "heights" offered them by God and began retreating to the bottom of the universe, just this side of nothingness—hell was already a reality. This hell is what theologians call the state or condition of hell, as distinguished from the place of hell. And this condition of hell came into being in the instant Lucifer said, "I will not serve," causing his created will and intellect to collapse upon themselves. We recall St. Augustine's declaration that sin causes a person to be *incurvatus in se* (curved inwards into oneself). Sadly, this hell all of us can experience to some extent, right here on earth.

Still, this is the earth, and not hell. The condition of hell is only on earth in the minds of those who have chosen it. Even when, like Job, we undergo sufferings in comparative innocence, these are of a different nature from the inner prison called damnation. For the Devil, however, that condition has become his permanent state of mind; and unless God has plans we are unaware of, the Devil cannot change his mind. But "the great dragon was thrown down, that ancient serpent, who is called the Devil and Satan, the deceiver of the whole world; he was thrown down to the earth, and his angels were thrown down with him" (Apoc. 12:9). Now if the Devil and his angels are on the earth, and the earth is not the place of hell, are they themselves not yet in the place of hell?

Grasping this distinction between state and "place" is of enormous importance for the understanding of demonic activity in this world. We need not enter into speculations about exactly where the place of hell might be—whether, as often believed in the past, somehow within the earth, or elsewhere in the cosmos, or simply in a superimposed dimension indiscernible to our mind or imagination in this life—we know that it is not here. The demons were hurled out of the inner court of the Holy Trinity, and God saw to it that they landed on the earth, on our poor orb. But why did he not send them all the way to hell (as a place) and preempt their terrestrial malice? Why did God allow St. Michael to cast this host of fallen spirits upon our green and otherwise so promising globe?

This is where the answer promised in the introduction begins to show itself. The fallen angels are *falling* angels. Since we poor earthlings also sinned at the beginning of our story, God has permitted Satan and his cohorts to serve the divine purpose of providing us with a long and difficult struggle before readmitting us to the lost paradise. This assignment gives the demons, as we shall see later, a kind of grace period; that is to say, they dread the final catapult into the definitive place of hell, however one interprets it. The simple reason for this is that once they land there, the most dreadful fate of all awaits them: inactivity. We recall Dante's chilling poetic vision of Satan *frozen* at the center of the earth. The only parts of him that moved were a pathetic, self-pitying tear, and the wings with which he tried in vain to free himself and produce warmth, only to spread the cold.

In the "place" of hell, the demons would be petrified face to face with their own despair. They would have none of the welcome distractions of wreaking havoc elsewhere, or of winning human souls as miserable companions. So just like the legion of demons driven by Our Lord from the Gerasene demoniac, they are willing to live even in a pig rather than be banished all the way down. "They begged him not to command them to depart into the abyss" (Lk. 8:31). That final exorcism is reserved for the end of time, and only Our Lord can perform it. But till then, the impure spirits are falling through our world. The only variables are how fast they fall, where they are able to hang on the longest, and when the will of

God ordains their definitive expulsion. What God does with them then is up to him.

The words of Our Lord in the Gospel are witness to this truth about falling. He takes for granted that a demon may be permitted to be exorcized to some other part of the earth, rather than all the way to the locale of hell, however we imagine it (see Mt. 12:43). Likewise, in the Church's official rite of exorcism, the third exorcistic prayer, in a mounting invocation of facts designed to terrify the possessing demon, finally invokes a truth that would inspire horror in any fallen spirit (the relevant phrases are highlighted):

> I adjure you, ancient serpent, by the judge of the living and the dead, by your Creator, by the Creator of the whole universe, by him who *has the power to consign you to hell*, to depart forthwith in fear.... To what purpose do you insolently resist? To what purpose do you brazenly refuse?... The longer you delay, the heavier your punishment shall be.

And then in the fourth prayer:

> An unquenchable fire stands ready for you and for your minions.... *Why do you still linger here?*... Begone, ✠ (sign of Cross) now! Begone ✠ seducer! Your place is in solitude; your abode is in the nest of serpents; get down and crawl with them. This matter brooks no delay; for see, the Lord, the ruler comes quickly, kindling fire before him, and I will run on ahead of him and encompass his enemies in flames. You might delude man, but God you cannot mock. It is he who casts you out, from whose sight nothing is hidden. It is he who repels you, to whose might all things are subject. It is he who expels you, he who has prepared everlasting hellfire for you and your angels, from whose mouth shall come a sharp sword, who is coming to judge both the living and the dead and the world by fire. Amen.

In the famous simple exorcism of Pope Leo XIII, for the use of bishops and priests in warding off general demonic influence, the same differentiation is made between the condition of hell, in which the demons already stand, and the abyss of hell, to which they have yet to be forever exiled. St. Michael is asked to "entreat the Lord of peace to cast Satan down under our feet, so as to keep him from *further* holding man captive ..." and that "the mercy of the Lord may quickly come and lay hold of the beast, the serpent of old, Satan and his demons, casting him in chains into the abyss, so that he can *no longer* seduce the nations" (*The Roman Ritual*, 1964 edition).

There is only one thing that can soothingly delay a given demon's measured plunge, and that is human sin. Every one of us who sins offers one more "handle" that will soon sport the grimy fingerprints of hell. The tactics of evil are basically quite simple: tempting us to sin.

The foundation-stones we offer for this kingdom are the fruits of our sins. But even we are not complete fools. The Enemy can lure us into all this only by convincing us that his labors are interesting and promising and, finally, that sin, instead of God, is the great mystery of the universe. He works day and night to make the depths of the abyss masquerade as a profundity of fascinating mystery, instead of a swamp of everlasting boredom. Even the Devil must delude himself into thinking he is entertained. To the damned, the deep things of Satan are a drag.

4

The "Deep Things" of Satan

AT THE BEGINNING OF THE APOCALYPSE, Our Lord instructs St. John to write to the angels of the churches in Asia Minor. In these letters, a wealth of guidance is offered to Christian communities of all times. Among other things, particular dangers are pointed out which lie in wait for all followers of the Lamb. For instance, we are warned against such evils as "the synagogue of Satan" (Apoc. 2:9, 3:9) and "the teaching of Balaam" (Apoc. 2:14). But it is perhaps in the fourth letter that we find the most summary description of the forces at work against our faith. In that letter, Christ commends as particularly praiseworthy those Christians who "have not learned what some call *the deep things of Satan*" (Apoc. 2:24). This in a way epitomizes the state of soul of those "who have not soiled their garments" (Apoc. 3:4) and are thus ready for the "marriage of the Lamb" (Apoc. 19:7). But just what are these "deep things of Satan," and why do they pose such a threat to the follower of Christ?

We saw in our last chapter that the demons are understood to be falling angels, and that their ongoing descent will terminate at the point of maximum distance from the throne of the Most High. We likewise identified as a plausible cause of their descent the refusal to accept the full consequences of the Incarnation. God's plan of lifting our lowly humanity into full communion with his own divinity, and placing Christ, with his glorified human nature, as head over all the Seraphim and Cherubim — including Lucifer — would have appeared too generous a promotion for man.

So rather than join in the wedding feast, the falling angels, like the prodigal son's elder brother, sulked. In an out-of-tune chorus, they chanted the words John Milton was later to put into Satan's mouth in his *Paradise Lost*: "Better to reign in hell than serve in heaven!" And down they fell to their new kingdom. There it was hoped, with Lucifer at their head, they could prove to God the possibility of working out a suitable beatitude of their own. And yet one thing was clear to them: it would have to be light-years away from the intolerable gaze of God's searching eyes. After all, "What fellowship has light with darkness?" (2 Cor. 6:14).

Falling down to the earth, and heading ultimately for the underworld, the demons did their best to make a virtue of necessity. Since they were falling further and further from the light of God's inexorable truthfulness (for "God is light and in him is no darkness at all" [1 Jn. 1:5]), one of sin's most recognizable achievements became second nature to them: self-deception. We know this experience well enough. The less we think of God, and the less we pray, the more skillfully we are able to evade and even deny truths we find troublesome. Distance from God's light and grace puts us at ease in the presence of duplicity. Our adeptness at self-deception begins to take on a certain professional polish, and finally, we are able to snuggle up with a purr to the most outrageous falsehoods.

"When anything becomes exposed to the light it becomes visible" (Eph. 5:13), St. Paul tells us. So, we flee the light, and our sins grow like toadstools in the dark. Apply all this to the demonic world, and you have the most dismal chamber of distorted mirrors ever designed. Our poor earth, still lying in "darkness and in the shadow of death" (Lk. 1:79), proved an altogether agreeable workshop for the projects of a fallen spirit (as it is for our own spirits when they fall). It was to this dark orb that God had banished him, mandating this exile as an appropriate punishment for those who had impugned the divine will.

In the darkness of our world, the Enemy of God set out to prove he could manage existence quite well without grace. Before long, he had won his first abject consolation. We can read about it in Genesis, chapter 3. The turning point lies in a single phrase: "And the woman said to the serpent..." That is all. Our fate was sealed once we agreed to dialog with Satan. The ensuing exchange is full of instruction in the psychology of temptation, and we shall return to it in the next chapter; but the mere fact that a human being agreed to talk to a fallen angel was the great inaugural mistake made at the dawn of history. The rest of our story, and the rest of the Bible, would have been but one overgrown footnote to the second verse of Genesis, chapter 3, if God had not intervened. But he did.

What has Satan been up to ever since he won our attention in the Garden? His most visible work has been inciting us to sin in very visible ways, such as murder, fraud, lying, adultery and thievery. Less visible maneuvers, through sins of the heart or organized evil in secret societies, have also occupied centuries of demonic industry. Both sorts of evil increase the handles of sin on earth, and thus serve well to further delay the demons' final descent. We shall deal with both these devices in the next chapter. But by following the reflections with which we began the present chapter, we might discern a far deeper inspiration of all demonic strategy. It could give us the master-key to uncovering the manifold tactics we will afterwards consider.

Satan's Burlesque of God's Mysteries

God Almighty is the ultimate Mystery. He is infinite, eternal and holy; he is all-knowing, wise and provident; he is just, merciful and loving; and he is all-powerful, strong and firm. "Can you find out *the deep things of God*? Can you find out the limit of the Almighty? It is higher than heaven—what can you do? Deeper than Sheol—what can you know?" (Job 11:7–8). It has been granted to man to gaze into these depths through the revealed mysteries of the faith. These are finally mysteries of God himself. Nothing else can ever be properly mysterious unless it participates in their mysteriousness. However, certain things can get deceptively close by sacrilegiously imitating them. And such travesties, of course, are a favorite pastime of God's enemies.

All Christian theology revolves around the inexhaustible content of its three principal mysteries. Though there are a number of ways to approach their meditation, the one I am choosing here may help us best to appraise "what some call the deep things of Satan." The three Christian mysteries are firstly, the mystery of the Most Holy Trinity; secondly, the mystery of the Incarnation and Redemption; and finally, the mystery of the Holy Eucharist. I am choosing here to highlight one particular aspect of all three mysteries, and the one which is most diligently counterfeited by the strategists of hell. It is an aspect which is most natively Christian, and most properly an attribute of the Living God and all that he does: the attribute of *fecundity*.

The genuine mysteries of God are so many aspects of his living, teeming fecundity. Even in the inner being of God himself, within the Most Holy Trinity, we find the ineffable mystery of eternal generation, a fathering forth of the Son from the Father, and the Holy Spirit proceeding from both. Within the indivisible unity of God's nature, three most holy Persons perfectly possess the one nature, and in the very act of possessing it are inseparably related to one another in their different modes of possession. This mystery of non-mathematical plurality in metaphysical unity has its inner dynamism in the fact that God is loving fecundity, and the generation of the Son by the Father is its necessary, never-ending expression. The Eternal Father is finally everyone's Father, the One "from Whom all fatherhood in heaven and earth is named" (Eph. 3:15). And the secret of this endless generation of life is the co-extensive divine mystery of love.

In the Incarnation we find God turning to his creation. He had produced this creation out of the pure abundance of his own love, and without the least constraint. He then showed his generosity in cascades of gifts. He gave to creatures their natural being as his first gift. When we rebelled against his second gift of grace, he looked about, as it were, for another kind of giving that could be granted to those who had rejected grace. Fortunately for us, a new species of giving did indeed emerge from the same fountain of fecundity: we call it *forgiving*.

Desiring our Redemption, the Son entered the world, and his Father now pronounced in time what he had forever proclaimed in eternity: "You are my Son, today I have begotten you" (Ps. 2:7). The created Humanity of Mary's Child was united with the uncreated Divinity of the Son, and in forgiving us our sins, the Father gave us his Son — the ultimate divine production, the most splendid of all his works, the unsurpassable gift from God's largesse of love.

But this is not all. Our Lord appointed priests for his Church and invested in them further productive powers, the powers of reconciliation and consecration. Through their sacramental words, sinners lose their sins, and the ordinary staples of human sustenance are changed into the very Humanity of Christ united with the Godhead. The now mysteriously glorified Body and Blood of Christ become present to his Church in a form that can not only be believed in as an object of faith, but also be taken into our still unglorified bodies as genuine nourishment.

All of these are mysteries of divine fecundity. They bubble over with life. Their mysteriousness is precisely that they derive exclusively from God, either by being the mystery of God himself, or by deriving from his divine magnanimity. They are, in summary: the Holy Trinity, God's inner mystery of eternal love and generation; the Incarnation (and connected therewith — both fore and aft — the Creation and the Redemption) as God's superabundant giving of life and love to beings of his own production; and the Holy Eucharist, God's intimate communion with his material creation, making even lifeless matter into a vehicle of sanctification.

Now if the Devil desires to "make himself like the Most High" (Is. 14:14), he must try to mimic these divine mysteries as closely as he can, and thus dupe gullible mortals into believing he has God-like powers. But he is intrinsically stymied in this effort. His greatest frustration is his total and inalienable sterility. St. Paul warns us not to take part "in the *unfruitful* works of darkness" (Eph. 5:11). Obviously, not being God, when he feigns to be a creator, he is doomed to failure, even fiasco. But he is so much smarter than we are — smarter, not wiser — and thus has little difficulty in convincing a good number of us that he has succeeded.

His triumphs lie in producing the misapprehension that he has created his own world, making himself into the principle of all that exists in that world. Now this demonic world really exists; in that sense, it is no illusion. It really is full of the one thing for which a creature, and only a creature, can take full credit: sin. The world of sin, in all its varieties, with all its tiresome degrees — limited in relation to the virtues, but still an impressive lot — is the *opus magnum* of the evil one.

But of all the sins he inspires, none is more blasphemous than that of arrogating to himself the adoration due only to the true and fruitful God. Thus, he typically demands some form of fornication as the token of our worship. Even more than *Rosemary's Baby*, fruitless fornication is the offering he most covets. And since our God-given fecundity is the endowment he in some ways most envies, he loves to lure us into debauchery and watch our seed spill and our wombs desiccate. However, should this enemy attempt to duplicate the loving act of Christ's Incarnation, Passion, Death and Resurrection, his travesty is easily exposed. He cannot handle an even remotely plausible mimicry of true love. It's a language he does not speak and can never learn.

A Christian mystery is burlesqued in all the forms of demonic "sacrament," from direct sacrilege in the infamous Black Mass, to the more common caricatures of the sacramentals in the usages of white and black magic: talismans, fetishes, amulets and, of course, the horoscopes neatly enshrined in all of our supposedly secular newspapers.

Our fundamental lesson from this chapter is that it is sin, and the thrill of sinning, that the Devil slowly unveils as his treasury of "deep things." He made them himself. Of course, we make our sins too; it's just that the Devil is so much better at it. And in one arrogant claim he is absolutely right: God can take no credit.

We are taught to thrill at the words: "Your eyes will be opened, and you will be like God, knowing good and evil." And despite all the wholesome distractions from sin provided by the Church, you too will "see that the tree is good for food, and that it is a delight to the eyes, and that the tree is to be desired to make one wise," so that you will grab and eat, and lo, "your eyes will be opened" (Gn. 3:5–7).

This is hell's only depth: the bottomless pit of sin. And like all abysses, it is both frightful and fascinating. Ever since these angels began slipping away from the one Mystery that is God, they made the troubling discovery that the further they fell, the more they lost all mystery of their own. In the end, the Devil is intrinsically un-mysterious. There is banality indeed in evil. Sin is ultimately Dullsville.

So, for this very reason the Devil works day and night to dazzle us into thinking that he himself is "the great mystery." This is at the basis of all the mystery cults, the secret initiations, the endless arcane symbols, numbers, codes, formulae and all the rest. With these and other devices, he endeavors to throw up a stupefying smokescreen in front of his naked, un-mysterious self. We humans are dull-witted enough that it often works.

We must concede: these things are deep indeed. And as you taste of the sins of the serpent, you will feel the tingling rush of the freefall, for now you too are tumbling headlong into the vortex of your very own, self-made abyss. But before we fall too far, let us examine the tactical offensives by which evil tries to make a world of its own. And let us see how these temptations lure us to the edge of a precipice and try to teach us, against all our saner instincts, not to be afraid to fall.

5

The Tactics of the Underworld

E ARE TOLD IN THE APOCALYPSE that after the Dragon had been hurled to the earth, his first enterprise was to pursue "the Woman." She, we recall, had given birth to a child, and the child had been "caught up to God and to his throne," and was hereafter beyond the Dragon's reach (Apoc. 12). This has been taken to symbolically depict the Ascension of Christ and the glorification in heaven of all those whom he saves by his redemptive death. St. John elsewhere affirms that "anyone born of God does not sin...and the Evil One does not touch him" (1 Jn. 5:18). The Woman, in turn, like so much in the Apocalypse, admits of at least three symbolic interpretations: the Chosen People of the Old Covenant (which brings forth the Messiah and his Mother); the Church of the New Covenant (which gives supernatural birth to all the saints); and ultimately, the Immaculate Mother of God herself.

Mary is, after all, the final blossom of the Old Covenant, and then as virgin Mother of the Church, the first blossom of the New. We shall see in a later chapter how the delicate foot of this Lady will one day crush the Dragon's reptilian head. But in the present chapter, we shall focus instead upon what the Enemy of

God has been up to ever since a further disappointment befell him. He discovered, to his great chagrin, that the immaculate purity of Mary, much like the glory of the Risen Christ, is also immune to his sordid enticements. Accordingly, Satan got "angry with the Woman, and went off to make war on the rest of her offspring..." (Apoc. 12:17). We can hardly claim neutrality in this war, for we and our children are the offspring referred to.

Just before the fall of the Dragon, St. John had heard a voice in heaven saying: "Woe to you, O earth and sea, for the Devil has come down to you in great wrath, because he knows that his time is short!" (Apoc. 12:12). The Devil's time is short—he is falling fast—and his plans to breed sinners for his infernal menagerie will have to progress swiftly. Accordingly, he is literally on the prowl: "Your adversary the Devil prowls around like a roaring lion, seeking someone to devour. Resist him, firm in faith, knowing that the same experience of suffering is required of your brothers throughout the world" (1 Pet. 5:8–9). Satan himself had to admit to being a vagabond, for when God questioned him at the beginning of the book of Job, "'Whence have you come?' Satan answered the Lord, 'From roaming about the earth, and walking up and down on it'" (Job 1:7).

The Benedictines are famous for their *stabilitas loci* (stability of place, meaning they are wed to a particular monastery, and renounce all the joys and distractions of mobility). The devils are just the opposite. Their temporary "rest stops" in and around ter-restrial sinners are mere postponements of their inevitable tumble. Even when they succeed in possessing a human being, either death or an exorcism will soon put an end to their strange vacation. They must keep on the move.

Our Lord himself said that "when the unclean spirit departs from a man, it roams through arid wastes searching for a place of rest and finding none" (Mt. 12:43). Although it is true that we Christians are also restless until our heart rests in God, and that we must "acknowledge that we are strangers and exiles on the earth" (Hb. 11:13), it is for reasons quite distinct from those of the demons. We "are seeking a homeland" (Hb. 11:14), and our days on earth are a pilgrimage. We may wander through deserts, like the

Israelites; we may retreat to the wilderness to pray, do penance and fight the Devil, as Christ himself, St. Anthony and the Desert Fathers did; but we are travelers following a careful roadmap. We move deliberately toward a place of heavenly rest prepared for us. In a word, we're not wandering, we're traveling.

The whole earth is a kind of restless no man's land for the Christian pilgrim, but there is a road passing through it and the New Jerusalem awaits us at the end of that road. The waters of our Baptism were the waters of the Red Sea, but not yet those of the Jordan; in other words, the sacrament of regeneration admitted us to a desert pilgrimage, and not yet to the land of milk and honey. The manna of the Eucharist will be needed in the desert till we find our way through to the Promised Land. But like the pilgrims of Chaucer's *Canterbury Tales*, amid the toils of our itinerary, we tell each other stories and will find much to enjoy during the trip.

The devils, in contrast, are not pilgrims at all; they are fugitives. For while they are falling from heaven, God only permits them to roam the earth for his own purposes. They serve his plan by testing and tempering the human race. They are the unwilling servants of the Providence they so despise. But all the while, they are dreading the moment when they too will have to go home. It is a kind of providential bargain God has struck with his rebel spirits: they can delay their final humiliation by serving as tempters of men on earth. Nonetheless, their consummate self-deception keeps them confident that, in the end, they will somehow be able to turn the tables on God.

We shall now have a look at the war that is waged against the offspring of the Woman. Not everything is chaotic in this altercation; there is strategy in the Satanic. If we look closely, we can espy order in the tactical offensives of the enemies of God.

The Three Basic Tactics of Hell

We have seen that the fallen angels abandoned the circle of God's plans, particularly that of the Incarnation, and are intent upon designing a new world according to their own projects. We also saw that they are constrained to seek various means of mimicking God's abundant fecundity. By that road alone will they be able to fashion a credible counterfeit of the life and works of a true God. Anything less would betray their limitations as creatures and expose their sham to the world.

This means, of course, turning the whole universe upside down. Since they are heading for the very rock-bottom of creation, they do their best to make it look like the very summit. One way to accomplish this is to deceive themselves into thinking they are climbing. "I will ascend to heaven; above the stars of God I will set my throne on high; I will sit on the mount of assembly in the far north; I will ascend above the heights of the clouds; I will make myself like the Most High" (Is. 14:13–14). The deep things of Satan love to masquerade as high things. One is reminded of the cartoon showing a turtle flipped on its back, looking into the sky and proclaiming: "I am flying!"

The Devil is the Ape of God, we say. And God is a Father. Thus, from his infernal factories, Satan begins to produce his own children. God has a Son, so he will have sons too. He is already the "Prince of this world" (Jn. 14:30) and has legions of demons under him (Mk. 5:9). But he wants a bigger family, full of those human animals God seems to have taken such a shine to. To this end, he mimics his hated Creator. God our Father tried us at the beginning of time, to invite our love of God; Satan will tempt us to the end of time, to incite our hate of God. Thus, the Prince of this world is eminently known as "the Tempter" (1 Thess. 3:5).

As the Tempter, he spawns the only children within the power of his mock-fertility, the Frankenstein monsters of hell: sinners. St. John writes: "He who commits sin is of the Devil; for the Devil has sinned from the beginning" (1 Jn. 3:8). Our Lord had these words for a few such sinners, addressed to some of the Scribes and Pharisees: "You do the works of your father.... You are of your father the Devil: and the desires of your father you will do. He was a murderer from the beginning: and he stood not in the truth, because truth is not in him. When he speaks a lie, he speaks of his own: for he is a liar, and the father thereof" (Jn. 8:41–45).

Later on, in the Apocalypse, St. John completes this portrayal of the Devil's work by calling him "the Accuser of our brothers, he who accuses them before God day and night" (Apoc. 12:10). So the princely Tempter of this world is 1) a Murderer; 2) a Liar; and 3) an Accuser. We shall follow these shameful titles in sequence as a helpful means of outlining the tactics of the Ape of God.

The Tempter

Father Frederick Faber called temptation the raw material of glory. And it can be raw indeed, as we know too well. But what he is trying to say is that the vexing attractions and enticements that afflict us can be effective catalysts for strengthening our love for God. That is why God permits temptation to begin with. Our difficult resistance when we do not fall, and our humiliation when we do, are both capital means of educating a fallen human race in the virtues it lost through sin.

The Devil, quite unwittingly (remember his consummate self-deception!), has been enlisted by God into this office of humanity-improvement. Reread the first chapter of the book of Job. God permits Satan to do all sorts of even violent things to us, but all the time the divine hand determines the measure and gives the signal when to stop. All the affliction, however incomprehensible to our minds, is motivated by the pedagogical love of God. Whether he directly punishes us through his holy angels, for "whoever is dear to me, I reprove and chastise" (Apoc. 3:19), or simply permits fallen spirits to tempt and afflict us, it is a father's stern love that is at work.

Temptation is an allurement to sin, whether it merely accosts our senses and emotions (as in Christ's temptation in the desert, to which we will return), or, as with all born in original sin, it actually attracts the will. The spiritual tradition of the Church has identified three principal sources of such allurement: the world, the flesh and the Devil. God may try us by permitting afflictions and sufferings to befall us (as befell the Israelites in the desert), but "let no one say when he is tempted, 'I am tempted by God'; for God cannot be tempted with evil and He himself tempts no one; but each person is tempted when he is lured and enticed by his own desire" (Jas. 1:13–14). God permits these three sources of temptation to operate, but he and his holy angels never directly attract our wills to sin. They are incapable of the malice such seduction would require.

And we must take care to remember that the Devil is not always the immediate agent of all temptation. The world and the flesh can work directly upon our wills without him. The things God created are natural goods and exert a legitimate attraction on our will. But—and here's the rub!—we are free to desire them in a disordered way, and the attraction of our weakened will toward such disordered possession is the temptation of the world. It is much the same with the flesh. The legitimate pleasures of marital, procreative love ought to be attractive to every red-blooded mortal. But here again, and even more so, disorder easily transforms healthy desire into disordered concupiscence.

Having made these qualifications, we still must recognize a certain preeminence of the Devil as Tempter, even regarding the world and the flesh. He may not be the immediate agent of their tempting force in every case, but very often he is pulling some strings backstage. We may suspect that behind most enticements to greed or impurity, some larger demonic strategy is also on the table.

The Enemy may fill our imagination with images of forbidden possessions or pleasures and allow them to work on us with their own native fascination. But he can still be the instigator. His greater triumphs, which lie in pride and disobedience, are often gradually approached by weakening our wills through preliminary sins of lust and covetousness. In this way he who is Prince of the World will work through that world to get at our wills. Did he not boast to Jesus that the whole world "has been delivered to me, and I give it to whom I will" (Lk. 4:5–6)?

When we speak of the Devil as the direct and immediate tempter, we are referring to his most characteristic enticements, those to pride. This, of course, is his special hobbyhorse. In promoting temptations by way of the world or the flesh, even if the victim is not "promoted" to the higher spiritual sins, he reluctantly settles for these lesser conquests; at least they keep his booty away from God. Still, when he zeros in on genuine pride, he knows that human recruits in this sin of sins will be the most coveted trophies in his kingdom. After all, he himself fell through pride, which is "the beginning of all sin" (Sir. 10:13), and his great self-deception began with pride ("The pride of your heart has deceived you" [Ob. 1:3]), so it is only logical that he would put a special premium upon success in this area.

But all sins are welcome in the brave new world of hell, so long as they are odious to God the Father. "All that is in the world, the lust of the flesh and the lust of the eyes and the pride of life, is not of the Father but is of the world" (1 Jn. 2:16). And so we are beginning to see a certain order in the Enemy's tactics of temptation.

The Murderer

Sins of the flesh have to do with abusing our life-giving powers of procreation, surrendering to lust irrespective of the responsibilities of life. But the Devil is, as we saw above, the Murderer, and promotes not only the many homicides that result from the passions of disordered sexuality, but even more directly, all sins against procreation and our God-given fecundity.

We counter these temptations by submitting our life-giving powers to the commandments of the one who gave us life. Chastity is but the order of reason in the area of the sexual appetite. As history has documented time and again, disorder in this area is the most destructive of all, for it undermines the very support-system of life itself. There are usually three steps in anti-life tactics: a) indulgence and excess: a lack of measure even in the legitimate uses of the procreative faculty; b) perversion: excess eventually brings a sense of glut, and the appetite seeks variety to keep the pleasure coming; and c) self-destruction: the sterile, draining effects of perversion leave a person feeling like a squeezed-out orange, and not infrequently, thoughts of the ultimate act of passion may logically arise: the destruction of life, even suicide.

Christian tradition has wisely followed the New Testament counsel of inviting some to observe virginal chastity, not because sex is bad but precisely because it is so good. Only good things can bewitch our will, and something so good as that which passes on the current of life can easily get out of hand. Furthermore, only good things can be sacrificed. Paradoxically, no higher tribute has ever been paid to our procreative powers and the pleasure they bring than on the part of those who sacrifice this intimate endowment by giving it back to God.

Our Lord's first temptation in the desert had to do also with the flesh, although certainly not with concupiscence. The Devil addressed his hungry body, after a forty-day fast, and urged him to use his powers to turn stones into bread. This too would have been an unnatural pandering to the flesh, outside of the divine order of things. Accordingly, Christ retorts: "It is written, 'Man shall not live by bread alone, but by every word that proceeds from the mouth of God'" (Mt. 4:4). Bodily mortification and fasting are here coupled with the nourishment of God's Word. ("You are clean, by the Word which I have spoken to you" [Jn. 15:3].) For the chaste — and even more especially for the virginally chaste — the pure, teeming outpouring of God-willed life is kept in a strong and lasting current by the firm riverbanks of God's law and God's Word.

The Liar

We don't live by biological life alone, but also by the truth of living words. Sins of the world (lust of the eyes) have to do with denying the fundamental truth of creation: that "in the beginning, God created the heavens and the earth" (Gn. 1:1), and that through the Word "all things were made, and without him was not anything made that was made" (Jn. 1:3). "It is he that made us, and we are his; we are his people, and the sheep of his pasture" (Ps. 101:3). We did not and cannot create a world, much less make our own laws for it. "The world was created by the Word of God" (Hb. 11:3, *passim*). And "in him all things were created, in heaven and on earth . . ." (Col. 1:15).

It is in denying the creation, and with it the role of the Incarnate Son of God, that the Devil exalts himself as the great and unequaled Liar. Only by negating the humbling truth that he is but a creature of God, made from nothingness, and further by contradicting the Incarnation, can he continue his vast self-deception. As a consequence, he who "has nothing to do with the truth, because there is no truth in him" (Jn. 8:44) will seduce some into believing that he is the real maker of the world (the so-called Demiurge).

In some versions of his deception, it may even be taught that the world is therefore as evil as he is. The many varieties of Gnosticism and Manicheism sprout from this illusion.

St. Paul already knew of these deviations. He writes of some "giving heed to deceitful spirits and *doctrines of demons*, through the pretensions of liars whose consciences are seared, who forbid marriage and enjoin abstinence from foods which God created to be received with thanksgiving by those who believe and know the truth. For everything created by God is good..." (1 Tim. 4:1–4).

A more unmasked assault of lying is directed by the Devil at Christ himself. For though Our Lord did not come to save the world in the sense of the present order of things, still very much under the regency of Satan ("I am not praying for the world, but for those You have given me" [Jn. 17:9]), he did come to save the world in the sense of human and material reality as it was intended to be. God "created all things that they might exist" (Wis. 1:13), and "he so loved the world that he gave his only Son..." (Jn. 3:16). So the lying spirit that had so often been put into the mouths of false prophets in the Old Testament utters his final and most blasphemous lie as the Antichrist.

St. John writes: "By this you know the Spirit of God: every spirit which confesses that Jesus Christ has come in the flesh is of God, and every spirit which does not confess Jesus is not of God... By this we know the spirit of truth and the spirit of error" (1 Jn. 4:2–6). "This is the Antichrist, he who denies the Father and the Son" (1 Jn. 2:22).

The Church has countered this great lie by encouraging the observance of evangelical poverty. In poverty, the Christian acknowledges that the world belongs to God, not to him, and that he is placed in the world only as its steward, to "till it and keep it" (Gn. 2:15). Resisting the lust of the eyes and the treasures of the world, he does his work quietly, awaiting the end of his life with surrender. The only treasure of such a soul is Christ, for he "confesses that Jesus Christ has come in the flesh" (1 Jn. 4:2). Ever since that happened, as St. Jerome said so long ago, the world has been over. The present order of things in this world is no longer Paradise, and not yet the New Jerusalem. In the words of the Second Vatican Council: "The form of this world, distorted by sin, is passing away (cf. 1 Cor. 7:31) and we are taught that God is preparing a new dwelling and a new earth in which righteousness dwells..." (*Gaudium et Spes*, n. 39).

Christ was also tempted in the desert on this point. The Devil urged him to use his powers over the physical universe and fly from the top of the Temple. Even if the Lord had these powers, he would not use them outside the divinely willed order of his mission. The first temptation had been for bread, the feeding of the flesh; this second temptation was for power, the flexing of muscle.

This is the presumption with which we reach recklessly into God's creation, trying, whether with ancient magic or with modern technology, to force it to obey us rather than God. This temptation, more than the others, goads us to tempt God himself, challenging him to match our act. Our Lord replies curtly: "Again it is written, 'You shall not tempt the Lord your God'" (Mt. 4:6–7). Finally, we are living a lie if we pretend, like the Devil, to be masters and possessors of nature.

The Accuser

The most native sins of the Devil (pride of life) are not so much directed against life and the body, as in his efforts as Murderer; nor are they principally concerned with the word and the creation, as in his work as Liar. No, his innermost concern is with pride, as we have already seen. Pride has as its immediate victim the virtue of humility, but as its ultimate victim, the growth of love. We shall see in a later chapter that in the last analysis, the fallen angels have no understanding of love at all. They are immune to its penetrating power. The pride they stimulate eradicates charity from the soul, making it docile to demonic influence. They are fighting love without really knowing what it is that they are fighting against. It is enough that its elimination serves their purposes.

But if it is not as Murderer, nor as Liar, that the Devil contends with charity, what Scriptural title can we give to this work? The one that fits is the third epithet we mentioned above: the Accuser. But what are we accused of, day and night, before the throne of God (Apoc. 12:10)? The answer is simple. We are accused of being hopeless sinners, just like the Devil! The Enemy fills us with despair and persuades us to doubt the mercy and love of God. He portrays the very idea of forgiveness as a colossal hallucination, designed to deceive us into becoming revolting peons of the Almighty.

We should bring to mind from our catechisms those terrifying "sins against the Holy Spirit," which, according to common teaching, are unforgivable. Such stern language is only used because it derives from the very words of Christ: "Whoever speaks against the Holy Spirit will not be forgiven, either in this age or in the age to come" (Mt. 12:32). The catechism went on to explain that these sins were unforgivable only because they so dispose our wills that we refuse the graces of contrition and pardon. As we saw before in our reflections on perdition, such a sinner would be one who locks the door of his soul from within, such that no one from without could unlatch it.

The similarity between those sins and demonic sin is all too clear. When the Devil succeeds in accusing us so well that we truly believe we have become like unto him, we may then despair of God's love, as he does; and thus, we feel confirmed in our obstinate perseverance in what we know to be sinful. There appears to be no hope anyway. These are the quintessential demonic sins rooted in a deep pride in our own powers, and a refusal to trust in a God we cannot understand and whose offer of pardon seems a cynical ruse.

The Church has countered all these attacks of pride, uncharitableness and rebellion with her warm encouragement of the vow of obedience. Our Lord was "obedient unto death, even death on the Cross" (Phil. 2:8). By that obedience, he won our salvation. Freedom *from* obedience, on the other hand, is the supreme delusion. We have freedom of choice, of course, but it cannot choose between obeying or not obeying, but only between competing acts of obedience. We can choose to obey that which is above us, and that makes us free; or we can choose to obey that which is below us, and that puts us in bondage. One way or another, however, we *will* obey.

The only way we can escape the persistent accusations of the Accuser is by taking loving refuge in the abundant love of God.

One might wonder why Psalm 136 keeps repeating, like a broken record, "for his steadfast love endures forever"—in all, 26 times! And other psalms beat the same drum. Only by praying much and deeply does this confidence grow in our hearts and the assurance of God's forgiveness become for us a tranquil conviction.

The Devil, it is true, offers us the whole world if we will only fall down and obey him. But he will turn on us in the end, and ridicule our subservience, accusing us of having finally been made over into his image and likeness. After he had taken Our Lord upon a high mountain, he made his last grand sales pitch: "'All these things I will give you, if you will fall down and worship me.' Then Jesus said to him, 'Begone Satan!' for it is written, 'You shall worship the Lord your God and him only shall you serve'" (Mt. 4:8–10).

Here is a small chart to help impress these demonic tactics on our memory:

Temptation of Christ	Our Temptation	Devil as	Victimized	Evangelical Counsel
Bread Temptation	Lust of Flesh	Murderer	Life	Chastity
Aviation Temptation	World	Liar	Word (truth)	Poverty
Adoration Temptation	Devil (pride)	Accuser	Love	Obedience

This scheme is only meant to assist our meditation. In reality, the tactics of the Enemy often grow quite disordered during the battle. He lacks a strong principle of inner order. He is not really *for* anything (not even his own self, which is afflicted with self-loathing); he is just against God. His attacks often change, his instruments vary, and we will never be able to make a definitive map of what he does. But there is far more design in his campaigns against God than many of us would like to believe. Nonetheless, of far greater importance than the study of the enemy's strategy is the use of Christian countermeasures, and above all, the deployment of the ultimate Christian camouflage. To these we now turn.

6

Christian Counterattack
and Camouflage

POPE ST. JOHN PAUL II, IN HIS HOMELAND
of Poland, had painful personal experience of the wiles of
both Nazi and Communist. He could hardly be naïve about
the need to arm oneself morally against evil. At his visit to the
sanctuary of St. Michael the Archangel at Monte Gargano, Italy, in
1987, the pope assured us that "this battle against the Devil...is
ongoing, because the Devil is alive and at this moment working in
the world.... For this the Apostle to the Gentiles puts Christians
on guard against the snares of the Devil and his many satellites,
when he exhorts the inhabitants of Ephesus to clothe themselves
with 'the whole armor of God, that you may be able to stand against
the wiles of the Devil.'"

What sort of equipment belongs to this whole armor of God,
and how do we use it? In this chapter we shall have a look at the
spiritual arsenal available to us. The weapons can be classified
under three main headings: 1) the frequenting of the Sacraments;
2) the pious use of the sacramentals; and 3) the strategic use of
the ultimate Christian camouflage.

The Frequenting of the Sacraments

Through Baptism, with the attendant exorcism prayed by the priest over the candidate (and the even more extensive exorcistic measures taken in the rites of the restored catechumenate), we are positioned for the first time within the supernatural context of Christian life. The infusion of sanctifying grace into our souls frees us from the power of original sin, and for a time, we become truly, objectively and intrinsically holy. Christian Baptism is the most powerful rite of passage on the face of the earth. "Having been delivered from the powers of darkness through the sacraments of Christian initiation" (*Ad Gentes*, n. 14), the "light that shines in the darkness" (Jn. 1:5) has "called us out of darkness into his marvelous light" (1 Pet. 2:9). Made into a living member of his Mystical Body, his life courses through our souls as a transcendent dimension of our natural life. Just as if we too had been not only created but also generated by God the Father, the claims and rights of inheritance of a true adopted child are ours.

Baptism, however, with all its hell-harrowing power, is not the finale of the symphony of salvation, but only the overture. Baptized babies will have to mature supernaturally, just as they will naturally. The Sacrament of Baptism lays the groundwork for our definitive emancipation from the Devil, but it does not seal that victory (except for those innocents who die before the age of reason). In the usual course of things, Christ's historical victory over Satan can become your personal and eternal victory only through the use

124

of your free will. And one of its noblest uses will lie in choosing to use the Sacraments.

A whole complex of further, post-baptismal Sacraments was instituted for the purpose of nourishing and protecting the fundamental graces of our new birth and assisting them to attain their ultimate and irrevocable coronation in future glory. Unlike the grace of Baptism, which, except for converts, is normally received independently of our free will (though by no means against it), the use of the other Sacraments is largely a matter of individual choice.

Beyond the youngster's dutiful reception of Confirmation and the Church's minimal precept of the Easter duty, we find ourselves quite at liberty regarding how often we communicate and how often we confess, and whether or not we wish to respond to vocations to the married or clerical state. Even in the mental confusion of our deathbeds, the ministering priest endeavors to detect a decree of our still sovereign will, before giving us the greatest parting gift the Church has to offer.

Now since our Christian life is on the battlefield we have already described, and the Enemy is quite intent on seeing that the seal of Baptism becomes a mark of mockery in hell, we are fools if we do not reach often and fervently for these God-given means of grace. By them, we feed our struggling souls for the contest, heal them from battle wounds, and fortify them for the last knock-out fight of death.

There is no more efficacious protection against any demon than a clean, shining conscience. This power of ours stretches itself in the sun of grace like a spiritual antenna capable of picking up the lightest whispered warnings of our guardian angel. Now to keep this antenna fully extended, no hours of ascetic effort can match the efficacy of one thoroughly honest and thus thoroughly humble confession. We shall have occasion to return to the subject of the Eucharist in the closing chapters. Here let us only note that the joint force of Confession and Communion sets in motion an intensity of spiritual growth that, together with maturation in the virtues, makes our spiritual immune system virtually impenetrable.

The Pious Use of the Sacramentals

The new Code of Canon Law defines sacramentals as follows: "Somewhat in imitation of the sacraments, sacramentals are sacred signs by which spiritual effects especially are signified and are obtained by the intercession of the Church" (canon 1166). Vatican II's *Constitution on the Liturgy* also asserted that "by them men are disposed to receive the chief effect of the sacraments, and various occasions in life are rendered holy" (*Sacrosanctum Concilium*, n. 60).

A decline in the proper use of the Church's numerous sacramentals has honeycombed our lives with little passageways for the gatecrashers of hell. Back when holy water was used in most Catholic homes, scapulars and miraculous medals were around thousands of necks, priests frequently and gladly gave their sacerdotal blessing, and chaplets jingled in pockets at least as much as car keys — back then, most of those little doors were kept shut. Some of them were even slammed shut, as when a priest performed the simple exorcisms recommended by Leo XIII. But today we are all scared like rabbits that someone might call us superstitious. So, we leave the doors open, and the gatecrashers soon show up.

The Church's careful theology of sacramental signs is designed to keep a proper Catholic use of sacrament or sacramental from easily falling into abuses. Of course, there can be and is an improper, non-approved use of sacramentals, and we must concede the damage done by those who use medals like fetishes, or who think a St. Christopher's statue on their dashboards will secure angelic protection while they break the speed limit. Long ago the

Romans coined the phrase: *abusus non tollit usum* (abuse does not preclude use). Whatever the sacramental sign used, the honor shown is never intended for the sign but for the signified, that is, for God and his holy ones. We should always keep that in mind.

The Church has never precisely defined the classes of sacramentals or enumerated them as she has the sacraments. One reason is because there are so very many of them. Only by taking the Code's definition and looking at *The Roman Ritual* can we gain a certain overview in the matter. In a broad sense, sanctified times and places, embracing the whole liturgical calendar and all the churches and shrines of the Catholic world, qualify as sacramentals, for they are signs of spiritual effects due to the Church's intercession. It was her intercessory authority before God that established them. Thus, the observation of feast days and the visiting of approved shrines both sanctify the faithful and serve to protect them from inimical attacks.

However, the more restricted, and more common, understanding of sacramentals identifies them rather with certain actions, words and objects to which the Church has attached an efficacious communication of grace. They do this by virtue of her powerful intercession before God, and not merely on the merits of the individual user. Private prayer of personal design, for example, is good and meritorious. But its value lies purely in the love and effort you invest in it. The use of the rosary, on the other hand, or the devout wearing of the brown scapular obtain an effect beyond that which relies on your own devotion. They are sacramentals, and when they are used with at least a minimum of requisite piety, the whole Church stands behind the user with her intercessory power.

Most sacramentals fall under the broad category of what are termed benedictions or blessings. In 1985, the Vatican published the revised *De Benedictionibus*, with 500 pages of the Church's official blessings. One look at this tome is enough to convince anyone that blessings were not at all jettisoned by the liturgical reform. Having one's home blessed, for example, is an efficacious means of securing abundant angelic help in warding off multiple afflictions to which family life is so often subjected. Libraries, travelers, technical instruments, animals and farm fields are among the many potential recipients of one of the Church's official blessings.

It would be beneficial if more priests would limber up their blessing arm and offer this powerful sacramental to their spiritual children. What is so superstitious about making the sign of the Cross with a specially consecrated hand over one of the embattled children of Adam? Ask your priests for this blessing from time to time; there must be a few around who are just waiting to be asked. The other principal sort of sacramental is the exorcism. This subject merits another book, but let us simply complete the list by encouraging the faithful to learn the use of little exorcisms, such as the St. Michael's prayer, or some of the others given at the end of this book. Leave the big cannons for the bishops and priests, but today you do need a pocket pistol. Have it ready.

The Ultimate Christian Camouflage

The regained innocence of a child constitutes the Manhattan Project of Christian strategy. Unlike the developers of the atomic bomb, however, the Church has never needed to occupy top-security hideaways in order to discuss the recondite formulae of the new ammunition. The Church has never needed to adopt an enciphered language in order to conceal the secret insights from its enemy's skillful decoders. Her strategy is unique in this regard. A couple of interesting crooks once discovered that the very best way to rob a department store would be to walk right in during business hours, and quite deliberately and naturally carry one item after another out of the store. The very obviousness of the action veils its underlying motive.

Or there is Edgar Allen Poe's tale of "The Purloined Letter," in which a much-sought letter is hidden from investigators by placing it in full view on the mantelpiece. Every corner of the dwelling is inspected, but the letter was not found, for it was carefully hidden right under the investigators' nose.

We can imagine the detectives of hell overturning the carpets of God's creation and sticking their noses into the furthest recesses of its structure, convinced that one day they shall find the real rationale behind the songs of martyrs and the strange fecundity of virgins. They have heard us use the word love, but they still cannot believe it is as simple as that. In the famous book of C. S. Lewis, *The Screwtape Letters*, the senior devil Screwtape gives some pointers about the Enemy (in this case, Christ) to the rookie tempter, Wormwood. In essence he tells him that all this talk about love must be a disguise for something else — "the Enemy must have some real motive for creating humans and taking so much trouble about them.... If we could only find out what he is really up to!"

Unfortunately for them, this is, for a fallen spirit, the ultimately inscrutable, imponderable, impenetrable secret. It does not and cannot make sense to them. The innocence of a child — and innocence when regained by an adult — seems almost extraterrestrial to them. Only those creatures who have freely given themselves in love to another person know the expansive wonder that unfolds in their hearts. Only they know why all the pain, frustration and anguish love often brings is a small price to pay for having one's heart opened to the fullness of reality.

The challenge, of course, is that you cannot truly get into love, without first letting love get into you. You must allow yourself to be possessed by someone other than yourself and submit yourself to someone and something your mind has not yet mastered, and indeed will never master. Most menacingly of all — at least for those who take pride in their self-control — you become vulnerable. All these prospects were perfectly horrible to Lucifer, so he did not let love in. As a result, he and all the hosts of hell who followed his example haven't the foggiest notion of why we all carry on so much about "this thing called love."

So, in summary: If you want to keep reasonably clear of the Devil in his overall schemes against the human race, frequent the sacraments. If beyond this, you wish also to bar off dozens of minor byways of his manifold mischief, make pious use of the sacramentals as well. But if you want to become virtually invisible to all the peering, prying eyes of every last one of the fallen angels, deploy heaven's ultimate camouflage. Grow in love and *become* a true child of God (I italicize "become" to remind us that we are not to remain children in the natural order but become children in the supernatural order; there's a difference).

It may sound corny to join in the song "All You Need is Love!," but if it is genuine love that is meant, the chant is theologically accurate. Just put it in perspective, and you will see why this is so. The sacraments have as their ultimate purpose our sanctification; and the summit of sanctity is perfection in love. All the sacramentals, as we saw above, have their principal purpose in disposing us "to receive the chief effect of the sacraments." Now nothing helps us to grow in charity more than the Holy Eucharist. And nothing bulldozes away obstacles to charity as do repentance and contrition in confession. And nothing can dispose us to worthily approach these two power-stations of grace as do the sacramentals.

When our motivations are not on the level of charity, but are interlarded with pride, impatience, lust and other aberrations, our plans lie open before the satanic surveillance of human conduct. The horned heads will start sympathetically nodding, muttering: "There you are, you little sneak!" We are back on their terrain again. They could expostulate for hours, even years, about the advantages of applied pride, justified impatience, legitimate lust and all the rest. They know exactly what you are up to. They will help you with all the marks of selfless generosity — until the payoff, that is. But make your overriding motive the love of God and neighbor, and a disturbed murmur will run through the ranks of your tempters;

your ascent to God will have caused you to vanish from their radar screen with a blip, and all the wiretaps of hell will find themselves short-circuited.

Let us make this our major effort: to grow, and then grow again, and then grow even more in charity. The theologians teach us that there is no objective reason that this love cannot reach out to infinity; its object is, after all, the infinite God. A fallen angel does not really know a thing about love, and one can imagine their puzzled faces squished up at the windows of the New Jerusalem, like little children watching adult romances. But we know what is going on. Even while sojourning in this crazy world, if we learn to faithfully live the fourfold love that is heaven's final secret—love of God, proper love of self, love of neighbor and, yes, love of enemy—we shall be walking like invisible men through all the riotous armies of hell.

7

On the Two Cities

"TWO CITIES HAVE BEEN FORMED BY TWO loves: the earthly by the love of self, even to the contempt of God; the heavenly by the love of God, even to the contempt of self. The former, in a word, glories in itself, the latter in the Lord." In this way, St. Augustine characterizes the two societies which grow throughout human history: one, the City of God, organized around the Word and will of God; the other, the City of the Earth, organized around the word and will of creatures (*City of God*, 14:28). Although the Church is clearly tasked by God with the construction of the holy city, Augustine makes clear that we belong to one or the other city through our loves, and not simply by virtue of our birth or our explicit religious affiliation. Many of pure will and honest mind will be on the holy side even if not in the Church; and many supposedly card-carrying Christians will find themselves on the other side. The demarcation of the two cities may at times roughly coincide with the division Church/State (as in the Third Reich or the Soviet Union), but even our Western democracies are not always nurseries of virtue. We shall attempt in this chapter to trace the approximate outlines of these two commonwealths and to understand, as best we can, how God's enemies often organize their followers here on earth.

We shall begin with a consideration of the City of God itself. It is, after all, the only one we are really interested in. The City of the Earth, the one still under the Prince of this World, as Scripture teaches, is at odds with God's City and draws its whole purpose from opposing it. Therefore, we must first back up and consider what God ever intended in building a city. Only then will we understand why the darker forces ever went to the trouble of setting up a shadow metropolis.

The City of God—which is simply a metaphor for the ultimate divine plan in creating the universe, with all its angelic and human citizens—was to fashion a place where God could dwell. Certainly his eternal, infinite life had no need of this dwelling, for "he who has his dwelling in heaven" (2 Mac. 3:9) hardly requires a home away from home in creation; but God's likewise infinite love invited him to make one. The greatest gift of his love to angel, man and cosmos was not the first gift of their very creation but the second gift of being honored by becoming a "holy dwelling of the Most High" (Ps. 46:5). And Paradise was its first realization.

Man's inaugural sin was a refusal to allow God to dwell in his own world. For as Creator and Master of that world, God had acquainted us with its rules. The rules were simple in the extreme: don't eat of the Tree of Knowledge. No roster of prohibitions here. Observe the one taboo, and you may frolic in the garden like children with the other fruits spread out before you like an arboreal banquet.

We are not misguided when we are told that the first eleven chapters of Genesis are deeply symbolic, or for that matter the entire book of the Apocalypse as well. Protology and eschatology—that is, teachings about the origins and about the ultimate consummation of creation—deal with distant protagonists and remote events. They do not permit the kind of literalistic depiction we enjoy in the historical parts of Scripture (from Abraham through the Acts of the Apostles). However, we are being misguided when someone tells us that by being symbolic, these narratives are not true, or only metaphorical, or even just parables like the ones Jesus told.

No, the Garden, the Tree and the Serpent in Genesis, and Babylon and the New Jerusalem in the Apocalypse, and all the rest, are true, deeply true—but so deep that only sacred symbols can have access to their content; even cameras could not have photographed their details, had they been available. Furthermore, the depth of the events symbolically presented is twofold: They are first of all very deep chronologically, either in the past or in the apocalyptical future, but also deep within the profundities of our very own souls. The events lie so profoundly rooted in time and in human nature, we easily lose sight of them. In these texts, we learn about what happened in the primordial past, or is to happen in the distant future. But we also learn what happens, sooner or later, in the depths of every human soul, once it is emancipated from the distractions of the present.

The Serpent had already been booted out of God's heavenly dwelling for refusing to obey a likewise simple rule. But now he is enlisted by God to be the agent of man's trial of obedience. We have already examined the course of this temptation, and how the Serpent's baited hook often gets firmly lodged in our jaw. The essential point to be grasped is that both the angels' fall and our own resulted in the inhospitable expatriation of God from the world he himself had made. He had ordained that he would only dwell in this world at our invitation. And we turned him down.

The rest of the story of salvation is how God enables us again to endure his august presence. After our first sin, the world no longer resonated with his special presence; it had grown spiritually desolate. But there were still spirits in residence. Like the deserted Temple of Jerusalem after the destruction, the world too no longer had "an altar in the city that is God's dwelling place" (Wis. 9:8). To its great dismay, it discovered that "for a long time she will be inhabited by demons" (Bar. 4:35). In the midst of this enemy territory which the world had become, God began instructing man on how to rebuild his dwelling. The ark of Noah, the new land of Canaan pioneered by Abraham, the small Ark of the Covenant in the desert and finally the large Temple in Jerusalem — all these were so many rungs up Jacob's ladder, back to the Source from which all homes come.

King David made the city of Jerusalem into the earthly City of God. There alone the sacrifice pleasing to the Most High was offered, and the long wait for the messianic fulfillment began. His son Solomon built the monolithic Temple, but its very magnitude easily dazzled the eyes of those who should have been "straining in watching for God's salvation, and for the fulfilment of his righteous promise" (Ps. 119:123). For they strangely overlooked the little town of Bethlehem (Mic. 5:2), and the Mother of God walked unnoticed through the very grandeur her Son was destined to inherit.

The name of Mary is a two-syllable summary of all that we mean when we say Paradise, Noah's ark, Ark of the Covenant, Temple, the dwelling place of the Most High and finally, the City of God. She who mothered the Church, and all its waters of grace in the New Covenant, is the one ocean into which all the rivers of the Old Covenant feed. The four rivers of Paradise splash at the garden of her purity. The Red Sea and the Jordan both are like the hems of her mantle, for those who first crossed them were looking for someone like her. And the rising tides of the Temple floods, once seen in a vision by Ezekiel (Ezek. 47), were a prophet's survey of the superabundant graces Mary would one day mediate to the City of her Son.

When "the Word was made flesh and made his dwelling among us" (Jn. 1:14), Mary became the tabernacle that, for nine months, shepherded within her doors the Presence — both then and for the years in Egypt and finally in the house of Nazareth. But then the day came for Our Lord to accompany his parents to Jerusalem and to set foot in his Father's House. This house was his Mother's towering predecessor, the Temple of Jerusalem.

After Our Lord began to grow into manhood, mystics recount that he started teaching Mary and St. Joseph. Thereafter he began his active mission, preaching and working wonders for three years. But all his sermons and miracles gathered like a tornado at the seaside of Caesarea Philippi, as St. Peter stared agape at his Master over the words he had just spoken: "You are Peter, and on this Rock I will build my Church, and the gates of hell will not prevail against it" (Mt. 16:16).

Was the City of God to be built upon this simple, unsteady fisherman? The glories of God's presence had passed from the enormous Temple through the narrow passage of Our Lady's holy womb, and now were to come out into the other half of history balanced on the "rock" of a man named Peter. Such was the foundation, but if he had known what was to be built upon this foundation in years and centuries to come, he would have been dumbfounded.

The very first recorded word of Our Lord after this unexpected appointment was a violent rebuke. And it was issued to no one less than St. Peter himself. The Master had begun unveiling the mystery of his coming Passion; but the poor fisherman was still grappling with the puzzle of his unexpected promotion. He found the prospect of Christ's early death an altogether appalling one: "God forbid, Lord! This shall never happen to you!" Christ, from whose mouth had once flowed the hushing power of the Beatitudes, turned with unusual fury toward his newly appointed vicar and let out the words: "Get behind me, Satan! You are a stumbling block to me; for you are not on the side of God, but of men" (Mt. 16:22–23). However, the words were in truth directed at Satan, who had begun to whisper his confusions into the ear of Peter. And what began with Peter would continue to bedevil the Church up to our own day.

The City of the Earth

We cannot even finish our outline of the building of the City of God without noticing the contrasting hammer-blows of another construction site. For at the very moment when Christ appoints his first vicar on earth, Satan's presence casts an ominous and surprising shadow on what one would expect to be a ceremonious and buoyant moment. The warfare we have so often referred to is here poignantly present. The next major step in the founding of the Church would occur in the Upper Room at the Last Supper. But even at this most solemn liturgical occasion, twice the Gospel makes mention of the Enemy of God. Once, of course, it is in one of the darkest of all sentences in the pages of Scripture. After Our Lord had indicated to St. John that it was Judas who was to betray him and did so by offering him a morsel of bread, we read: "Then after the morsel, Satan entered into him" (Jn. 13:27).

The passage continues: "So, after receiving the morsel, he immediately went out; and it was night" (Jn. 13:30). St. Augustine commented on these last three words, saying that "he who went out, was himself 'night.'" Judas had allied himself freely with that nocturnal conspiracy which, in the beginning, had been separated by God from the "day" of the holy angels (Gn. 1:4). After being called by God to the inner circle of the City of God, he chose to shift his citizenship to the other jurisdiction.

The second time the Gospel mentions the Devil at the Last Supper was just after the institution of the Eucharist, and with it, the ordination of the first bishops. Again, it is the beleaguered St. Peter to whom the darksome words are addressed: "Simon, Simon, behold, Satan demanded to have you, that he might sift you like wheat" (Lk. 22:31). Here, the Greek word for *you* is in the plural, for Our Lord is referring to Satan's designs to upset the College of Apostles and try thereby to undermine the foundation of the new City of God. In the next line, however, the *you* is singular, as Christ assures St. Peter, "I have prayed for you that your faith may not fail; and when you have turned again, strengthen your brethren" (Lk. 22:32).

Only Christ's prayer will support Peter through the terrible trial of the Passion. He fails miserably, as we know. But the prayers of Christ helped him to "turn again." Equipped with this new humility and trust in God, he and the Apostles learn that the architectural principle of God's new City will be neither the glorious splendors of the Temple nor the restored Eden of Paradise but instead the blood-soaked Cross of Golgotha. Hanging and dying on that Cross, the Lord takes the third step in founding his Church by entrusting to each other the one Lady and the one Apostle who had flanked his naked, impaled Body. Turning first to his Mother, he says "Behold your son." And then turning to St. John, he says "Behold your Mother" (Jn. 19:26–27). Shortly thereafter, the Messiah dies, and from his pierced side, the Blood and Water pour forth that Mary and John will mediate in their different ways, on to all the mothers and all the priests of the Church's history.

Satan, it would seem, walked away from Golgotha in a fit of consummate self-deception. Having rid himself of this pretended Messiah, he could now go about the building of his own city in peace. It took time for him to realize that he had unwittingly hewn the very cornerstone of the adversary's edifice.

With the sending of the Holy Spirit at Pentecost, the Risen Lord completed the founding of his Church. This fourth and last step invested the Apostles with "power from on high," which sealed their mission. In the Holy Spirit and through the mystery of the Church, they were to prepare men on earth for the final perfection of all creation in the New Jerusalem. This was to be the heavenly City of God, destined to unite angel, man and cosmos in the mystery of Christ at the end of time (Apoc. 21).

What is Satan trying to accomplish by tempting St. Peter to turn Jesus away from the Passion? What does he hope to attain by sifting the Vicar of Christ like wheat? We answered these questions some chapters ago. The fallen angels have been trying from the beginning to build themselves their own dwelling place. And they know that the Church, even more than the Israel of old, has been armed against them. And at last hell discovers that heaven's great weapon is the Cross. It saves man from Satan's sin. So, by seeding sin wherever he can and opposing the Cross, the Enemy is hoping one day to sift the works of Christ right out of creation. He knows that "the reason the Son of God appeared was to destroy the works of the Devil" (1 Jn. 3:8). So he, in turn, must destroy the works of God. And the only way to do that is to attack the Cross.

Satan's sifting will be nowhere so thorough as there where the wheat of the earth has quite literally been lifted to the Cross of

Christ. I refer to the Eucharist. The Church grew slowly to recognize the full riches the Lord had laid into this mystery, and soon the Sacrifice of the Mass became the central act in the construction of the Heavenly Jerusalem. The Mass is potent because the Victim offered is the Flesh and Blood of Christ himself, both of them immaculate gifts of Mary to our salvation.

So over against the Holy City of Jerusalem will be the unholy city of Babylon. And as God permits the demons to roam about the earth for the probation of man, he also permits the walls of Babylon to grow high and mighty. In this way the soldiers of Jerusalem may be galvanized into saints as they learn to defend the things of God. And again, it is sobering to learn that the "two cities" of Augustine are not two hermetically sealed domains — one holy and perfect and the other unrepentantly wicked — but rather two vocations, two callings, allowing those from either camp to fall into the contrary faction. Many outside the Church will bear the banner of holiness more than some within, and defections from the societies of iniquity will be more frequent than their former ferocity suggests. Remember the persecutor Saul, who became the Apostle Paul; and remember Judas the Apostle, who became Judas the traitor.

In order that we may gain a certain overview of the way in which underground activity has traditionally organized itself, and that we may be able to at least identify potential dangers in our own lives, a few headings of the way the terrestrial city is organized will be given. But ideas have consequences. We will first identify the ideas we must defend if our words and actions are to be rightly guided.

Three Ideas Under Siege

Many spiritualities are on offer these days. Quite a few of them claim to be from the mysterious East, but it's very hard to check their credentials without a considerable amount of study and prayer. Still, one can identify impending confusion and danger if one or more of three key ideas are in any way negated or even just marginalized. Without these ideas in full profile, Christian identity is either going or gone. But to be fair to India and China, these ambiguities can also infect the spiritual ways of the West.

We must pay close attention here. That these truths are absent or under siege may not be obvious at first. They may even be integrated one way or another into the vocabulary, or even the initial beliefs one is expected to espouse; but to be true to themselves they must stand not only as subsidiary components but as ultimates or absolutes, which in the Gospel they unmistakably are.

The three truths are as follows: 1) God and the creation are not the same thing; the creation comes entirely *from* God, is entirely dependent *on* God and is entirely ordered *to* God, but *it is not God*; 2) human beings are free in their moral choices, and their one life on earth is their decisive time of trial (however complex the process of death and the posthumous realms may be); and 3) persons (divine, angelic and human) are the highest realities that exist, are everlasting (the latter two having a beginning but no end), and their supreme fulfillment lies in a form of knowing that is inseparable from personal love. Against these truths stand all the countless, modulated forms of pantheism (or monism), determinism and Gnosticism.

For the Bible, for the Catholic Church, for the mainstream Western tradition, these truths are non-negotiable; all else we know about the universe can be harmonized with them, correlated to them and both shine light on them and receive light from them. But they are forever under attack. The details of our scientific and philosophical knowledge can be systematically sequestered from these primordial verities, working greater evil than any network of lies.

This is not to deny that there are scores of truths contained in the Eastern traditions and also in what in the West are known as esoteric associations, with their own mother lodes of lore. Both in Eastern traditions such as Hinduism, Buddhism and Taoism (to mention just the most prominent), and in Western lineages of Rosicrucianism, Freemasonry, Theosophy and Anthroposophy (again, to mention just the most well-known), we find high percentages of insightful cosmological, metaphysical, moral and mystical truth. The problem that arises from a Christian Catholic perspective is not just the falsehoods and even lies that often afflict those truths. More dangerous is the simple lack of order and perspective among those truths themselves.

Some of them are shared by the West already, such as many fundamental metaphysical truths and basic ethical precepts. The East also has a vast repository of what theologians call the primordial tradition (also called *philosophia perennis*, or *prisca theologia*), meaning truths still enduring from God's initial revelation to the first human beings. All that is true in these traditions, as the Second Vatican Council has made clear, must be welcomed into the larger context of Christian truth, that "whatever is found in the minds and hearts of men, or in the particular customs and cultures of peoples, far from being lost is purified, raised to a higher level and reaches its perfection, for the glory of God" (*Ad Gentes*, n. 9).

But the same Council warns us that "very often, deceived by the Evil One, men have become vain in their reasonings, have exchanged the truth of God for a lie, and served the world rather than the Creator" (*Lumen Gentium*, n. 16). The purification of these traditions, referred to above, is for the glory of God indeed, but also "for the confusion of the Devil" (*Lumen Gentium*, n. 17). We must therefore be clear in our thinking when we confront such repositories of lore and practice.

The Occult, Witchcraft and All the Rest

Of a far less subtle nature are the more customary Western offerings of the occult: magic, divination, astrology, alchemy, palmistry, witchcraft, numerology and on through a long list of esoteric arts and associations. It covers just about every possible way of trying to appeal to the help of questionable sources — all linked in one way or another to the de-contextualized "knowledge" that is the specialty of fallen spirits — in order to gain "unearned wisdom," power or pleasure. Anyone who has frequented bookshops over the last few decades knows that what began, say, in the late '60s, as a shelf or two in the philosophy department labeled "Occult" has recently swollen into a whole department of its own. Today the name used may be (inaccurately) "metaphysics," or some other appropriation of classical terms ("alternative spiritualities," "New Age," "esoterica," etc.), but usually it will be neatly separated from Christian literature, on the one hand, and more serious academic philosophy, on the other. Serious scholarship about Eastern thought and religion might even constitute a further subdivision.

The Builders of Babylon

There is finally a golden, or better, brazen thread that runs through many esoteric doctrines, secret societies and all the disarrayed assortments of occult arts. It is the fact that they are all, directly or indirectly, in the employment of that other city. One famous secret society expressly honors as deity "The Great Architect of the Universe." If they are only interested in building the same City that the Church is building, which uses "that living stone, rejected by men but in God's sight chosen and precious" (1 Pet. 2:4), namely Jesus Christ, why is there a long history of conflict between them and the Catholic Church? The matter is complex and deserves longer treatment, but let us highlight only a few principles.

One reason for the uneasy relationship between Catholicism and secret societies is that the Church does claim a certain jealous exclusivity, which most proponents of perennial tradition will tend to de-emphasize in the interest of latitudinarianism. They will tend to accuse St. Peter of hyperbole (at least) when he says, "There is salvation in no one else, for there is no other Name under heaven given among men by which we must be saved" (Acts 4:13).

Occultists and New Agers often rhapsodize about the harmonies of the cosmos, the correspondences between stars and metals, between what is above and what is below, between macro- and microcosmos, between human organs and precious stones along with other symmetries and correlations. They might also speak of the great unifying mission of a supposed Age of Aquarius yet to come. What is a Christian to make of all this?

It is true that the fallen spirits have retained enormous knowledge and power over the physical, and indeed also what we might call the "psychic" or "subtle" creation. God appears to have permitted them, for the testing of humans, a large spectrum of influence in these matters. The Eastern traditions in particular are teeming with valid knowledge about the physical and psychic orders of reality. And in the West, these particular powers constitute the basis of all magical arts, and the various ways of playing on the interwoven tapestries of the cosmic design. The configuration of the stars at your birth; the way the lines in your hand are traced; your genealogical tree; energy vortices in the spinal column — these things and many more are indeed related to all sorts of subsidiary laws in God's creation. In the Middle Ages, Churchmen themselves often accepted this and tried to interpret them in harmony with the Gospel.

But by and large, unless we have a special vocation as exorcist or theologian, human days devoted to this occult domain — even if only with the intention of unmasking or criticizing it — easily become field days for the fallen spirits. Now if original sin had never entered the world, these dimensions of the cosmos and our relationship with them may well have been harmless, and formed an integral part of our ordinary lives. But since the fall, and because of the range of efficacy God has apportioned to the fallen angels, this area has been blighted with dangers and booby-traps. The Church has lent her voice to the repeated warnings against divination and consorting with strange spirits that one reads in the Old Testament. We most definitely have better things to do.

8

All that Glitters Isn't God

TWO DISTINCT CITIES ARE AT WAR. BUT the soldiers on either side are not always visible. "We are not contending against flesh and blood, but against the principalities, against the powers, against the world rulers of this present darkness, against the spiritual hosts of wickedness in the heavenly places" (Eph. 6:12). Distinguishing between belligerents is going to be trickier than it is in a merely human contest. It would be easier if all the holy angels wore khakis, and the devils were made to wear Halloween costumes. But as it is, angelic identification, at least for us mortals, calls for a relatively sophisticated art of discernment. For this reason, the spiritual tradition of the West has worked out a whole literature on the subject of the discernment of spirits. We shall attempt to draw together some of the more important rules in this chapter.

The root of the problem is, again, the deceptiveness of the Devil. The holy angels have no intention at all of misleading us. They may of course startle us. An angel could be sent to administer a divine punishment, as when David "lifted his eyes and saw the angel of the Lord standing between earth and heaven, and in his hand a drawn sword stretched out over Jerusalem." The thought may have crossed David's mind that a Devil, or a Goliath, could hardly be more alarming than this holy angel. But the angel is clearly on a divine mission. Once David does what God wants of him, the terror is gone and "the Lord commanded the angel; and he put his sword back into its sheath" (1 Chron. 21).

But are we not often in the shoes of Joshua instead, who "lifted up his eyes and looked, and behold, a man stood before him with his drawn sword in his hand; and Joshua went to him and said to him, 'Are you for us, or for our adversaries'" (Jos. 5:13)? Like Joshua, we too often have to ask, or at least in some way double-check to be sure we are in the presence of divine and not diabolical volunteers.

But how can we know with certitude that it is a holy angel? Why does St. John have to warn us "not to believe every spirit, but to test the spirits to see whether they are of God" (1 Jn. 4:1)? Fortunately, we are given a clue by St. Paul, but it is one that raises as many questions as it answers, for the Apostle writes that "even Satan disguises himself as an angel of light" (2 Cor. 11:14). Here one may well be tempted to complain that God, who circumscribes the area of legitimate temptation, could at least have forbidden the demons this particular ploy. What are we to do? It is hard enough to resist temptation when we know it is evil and that we are on the brink of sin. But how are we to resist when the tempter himself appears all decked out in garments that seem to have been selected from a heavenly wardrobe?

Before we continue, one qualification must be made with every possible emphasis. Although a demon can masquerade as an angel of light, his disguise is never foolproof. The discerning eye can always detect the telltale sign of evil, a kind of signature of Satan. We say, figuratively, that somewhere the cloven hoof is always sticking out. Still, although God does not give the Devil free hand in deceiving us, we are easy dupes to this imposter.

Despite the worry this may cause us, we must remind ourselves that God "does not do without cause all that he does" (Ezek. 14:23). If we think back, way back, all the way back to the Garden, God's logic in leaving us in this near dilemma will start to make sense.

Was not our original calamity the result of our presumptuous desire to "know good and evil"? And isn't that just what we got? The serpent was masquerading as an angel of God already in Eden. He had to. Would Eve have touched the apple with a ten-foot pole if Satan had said: "This is going to plunge you and your progeny into untold misery"? Cunningly, he offered us what appeared to be a treasure; a wonderful, sparkling treasure.

What could be wrong with a treasure of knowledge? We were given a mind and a body, and they were obviously given to us to be used. And what more fruitful occupation could our first parents have embarked upon than that of reaching out for this paradisiacal bargain: Godhood in one easy bite? "So when the woman saw that the tree was good for food, and that it was a delight to the eyes, and that the tree was to be desired to make one wise, she took of its fruit and ate; and she also gave some to her husband and he ate" (Gn. 3:6).

It is worth commenting upon that the three steps in Eve's fall follow the three sorts of temptation we outlined in chapter 5. She "saw that the tree was good for food" (the flesh, Our Lord's Bread Temptation, the need for chastity and order in the body's appetites); ". . . and that it was a delight to the eyes" (the world, Our Lord's Aviation Temptation, the need for a spirit of poverty); ". . . and that the tree was to be desired to make one wise" (the Devil, pride of life, Our Lord's Adoration Temptation, and our need for an attitude of obedience).

At any rate, "The eyes of both were opened." But here again, what is wrong with open eyes? Well, it depends upon what they open *upon*. "The knowledge of good and evil" promised by the serpent was in fact granted. The demons are meticulous in keeping promises and appointments; it is just that their interpretation of the terms always throws us. For the "knowledge" of the "*and evil*" part of the bargain turned out to be knowledge of themselves. "Know thyself," they may have snickered. Again, one wonders what could be wrong with that. But as Adam and Eve "know themselves," what is it they know? Here many of the earlier reflections of this book are flowing together as to a kind of common focus: "And they knew that they were naked."

147

You see, the Serpent kept his promise. We have really received the "knowledge of evil," and we are all still dizzy from our frequent stares down its black, bottomless vortex. And we know ourselves indeed, but as sinners. Now we know what sin is all about. We make our observations from the inside of the bottle. And, strange to say, we have grown restless over our new enrichment. When we hear the sound of God (Gn. 3:8), we are afraid, and we hide. We are naked, which means we have lost something integral to our dignity and feel ugly and exposed. We no longer know what we are all about. Nor do we really know where we are. And most puzzlingly of all, God does not seem to know either. "Where are you?" he asks Adam. We had disappeared into the darkness of sin. It is the worst of all fates to become invisible to God, like the foolish maidens to whom the Lord spoke: "Truly I say to you: I do not know you" (Mt. 25:12).

The "deep things of Satan" are the Gnostic apples of the Garden of Eden. They have opened our eyes upon the nothingness from which we came, and its dazzling darkness has spellbound us. We hide from God, we propagate, and we spread our race over the darkened earth, for we have "become like God, knowing good and evil" (Gn. 3:5). The joke, of course, is on us. Once again, we confirm the truth that sin is the only thing in the world you do not learn more about through experience. Evil is not a positive reality but a lack, a privation. You cannot really progress in the experience of sin. The more you sin, the less you understand what you are doing. In fact, this brings us a slight measure of consolation. It was the basis of Our Lord's gift of forgiveness in his first hour on the Cross: "Forgive them, Father, they know not what they do!"

Sin and evil cannot really be known, for they are blanks, holes and negatives. It follows that you cannot *fix* a sin or *solve* the problem of evil. All you can do is fill the hole with something real. If you go with a pair of shoes bearing holes to a cobbler, asking if he would please repair the holes, he might well respond: "I wouldn't even know how to repair a hole. I repair shoes." Our souls, fortunately, can be repaired; our sins cannot.

So here we stand, millennia later, riddled with the cavities of sin but still surviving and pressing toward various surrogate goals of our own design. Now it was into this Gnostic world of original sin that the God-Man Jesus Christ came, and what he brought was salvation from the prison of our knowledge of sin. Indeed, "The knowledge of Our Lord and Savior Jesus Christ" (2 Pet. 3:18) frees us from the "godless chatter and contradictions of what is falsely called knowledge (*gnoseos*)" (1 Tim. 6:20). What Christ brings are no new apples but rather "the full knowledge *of his will*" (Col. 1:9), through the "*love which surpasses all knowledge*" (Eph. 3:9). With this love he fills the holes in our souls. As we saw in the chapter on the two cities, the doctrine of demons is based upon knowledge independent of love. Christ's teaching turns that formula on its head. *He brings a love that produces knowledge.*

Now let us return to our original question. Why does God allow the Devil to disguise himself as an angel of light? We can now give an answer: to allow us to reverse our original sin. We wished to know good and evil—now we must learn the opposite angelic art; we must become "like the angel of God to *discern* good and evil" (2 Sam. 14:17). And God permits, in his educative love, that it not be an altogether simple enterprise. To allow Job to confirm our repeated observation, "The life of man upon earth is a warfare" (Job 7:1).

The Rules of Discernment

"Are you for us, or for our adversaries?" This is the question we must put to the spirit that wishes to guide us. But first of all, what are the kinds of spirits that can volunteer their services? The following does not pretend to be an exhaustive treatment of this difficult subject (an excellent book on the discernment of spirits is available by Fr. Tim Gallagher), but I shall try to give a manageable overview of three fundamental rules that cover most of our spiritual needs. But first, let us list the kinds of "spirits" we will have to discern, beginning with the big one: the human spirit (let us not forget this one—remember Enemy Number One!).

Our own fallen nature, moved by the four-fold wound of original sin (ignorance, malice, weakness and concupiscence), is quite capable of leading us astray. As we saw in our first chapter, the fact that "some have strayed after Satan" (1 Tim. 5:15) is possible only if our free will first chooses to follow the Enemy's promptings. The ignorance in our minds, the malice in our wills and the weakness and lust in our passions are all leaping with suggested spiritual pointers. They are like first-graders with hands high, anxious to answer the teacher's question. We must learn to sort out all these inside sources of influence from the other two kinds of spirit:

1. the spirits of heaven — either the Holy Spirit, Our Lord, his Mother, our guardian angel, the angels and saints;
2. then the demonic spirit.

The next question we must put is how these three kinds of spirits can affect us. What are we to be on the watch for? Traditionally, there are three of their effects that need to be especially heeded in spiritual discernment:

1. *consolations:* any one of the above-named spirits may produce a certain joy, illumination or peace in the soul, but for very different reasons, and with very different results.
2. *desolations:* any of the spirits may affect us also with the spiritual blues: dryness in prayer, discouragement, weakness in the face of temptations and a strong drift toward throwing in the towel.
3. *inspirations:* these influences may cast a light into our mind or energize our will to undertake some act or make some resolution. Here, as in the first two, any one of the three spirits could be at work.

In other words, my own disorderly human spirit could console me with a certain self-satisfaction (consolation) because I had sinned in a way that tallied with its own disorder. It could whisper in my ear that this thing is not really a sin at all, or at least not for you, or not today, or not…(so on and so forth). If my conscience is at all awake, it will pester me for having listened to that spirit at all. But the trouble is, I may think all the time that my good angel was at the other end of that communication. How can I tell?

Another example. I feel despondent and find prayer extremely distasteful. Upon examination of my conscience, I find no obvious sin that could account for such desolation. Is something wrong?

Need I change course? (Remember innocent Job?) The problem does not seem to be the work of the human spirit. So, there are two other possible explanations. Either the demon is showing his true self after a period of my supping on his sweetmeats or God is permitting a trial of aridity for my growth in holiness. Which is the case? Here are three rules that may be helpful.

First Rule: The Fruit Rule

"By their fruits you will know them," said the Lord (Mt. 7:16). Whatever the consolation, desolation or inspiration, watch whither it is tending. If it brings rotten fruit anywhere along the line, chances are you have been listening to the human or the demonic spirit and not to the angel. God's wisdom "reaches from one end to the other, and orders all things sweetly" (Wis. 8:1). If you are guided by the good spirit, there will be no sin, no tragedy, no foul smell of infernal presence anywhere along the road. There may well be discomfort, pain, trial, or in a word: the Cross — but it will all be of ultimate benefit if the help is coming from God.

If we begin to smell the rot developing, however laudable our intentions seem to be, we should beware. In all likelihood this case is one of the demonic spirit, which can even play on an imprudent fervor in pursuing excellent goods. With serious Christians, once he has failed to delude us into overtly sinful acts, the Devil will often have to do his best to corrupt good plans and desires. For this, we must learn to follow the story into the future and, as best we can, try to forecast the fruit.

Second Rule: The Foursquare Rule

The first rule covers all cases. The only trouble is that it must cover some of them only in retrospect, after the damage is done. While we are sitting among the debris, we sadly nod our heads and say: "I now know that act by its fruit." We cannot always wait for the fruit, nor are we always able to foresee its coming before we begin an important undertaking. Much has to be decided here and now. So, again, what to do?

The second rule is based upon two texts of the New Testament. The first is from St. Paul, who writes that "no one speaking by the Spirit of God ever says, 'Jesus be cursed!' and no one can say 'Jesus is Lord' except by the Holy Spirit" (1 Cor. 12:3). The other text is from the First Letter of St. John: "By this you know the Spirit of God: every spirit which confesses that Jesus Christ has come in the flesh is of God, and every spirit which does not confess Jesus is not of God. This is the spirit of Antichrist, of which you heard that it was coming, and now it is in the world already" (1 Jn. 4:2–3).

From these inspired words we have all we need for a litmus test to check interior movements of our soul, but without having to await or predict their fruits. This can be called the "foursquare rule," because its criterion is to determine whether the illumination or inspiration can be placed foursquare within the body of ortho-dox doctrine and practice. Does this little voice really say, "Jesus is Lord," and does it do this in the whole series of its planned acts? In other words, is there any detail of our Faith, any even minor moral commandment, any disciplinary injunction or anything whatsoever that belongs to the Gospel in its entirety, which this voice denies?

If so, the test is over. It is not from God. This does not mean that it has to be a full-fledged demonic temptation either. It may just be some of the flabby suggestions offered by our comfort-seeking human spirit. Or it may come from some of the compromising ideas in the clouds of heresy that are always hang-ing about; not so much wrong in what they say, but in what they do not say. God's inspirations, in contrast, come in full outfit. Each little voice from heaven will inevitably evoke a resonance of harmonized celestial tones. Truth is always symphonic.

An example: you get the idea of making a pilgrimage to the place of an alleged Marian apparition. Everything seems to be in order. There are Masses, confessions, prayer and all the trappings of approved piety. You want to go, you have the funds and the free time. But before making your final decision, you apply the foursquare rule in the discernment of spirits. You discover that one corner of your programmed pilgrimage cannot be pressed into the mold of orthodoxy: the local bishop has forbidden pilgrimages to this particular shrine. You go to Fatima instead.

Third Rule: The Familiarity Rule

The first two rules we derived from Scripture. This third rule comes out of the centuries of Christian spiritual experience and bears the stamp of a hundred saints' approval. Its most famous formulation is that by St. Ignatius of Loyola in the rules for discernment found in his magisterial *Spiritual Exercises*. Those twenty-two rules should be read carefully by every Christian endeavoring to advance spiritually. The distillation I should like to make is from the second week of the exercises.

We will call it "the Familiarity Rule" because it has to do with the kinds of spirits one is on most familiar terms with. One is looking here neither to future fruits nor to a squaring with dogmatic and moral criteria but instead to a more elusive, psychological state that accompanies the soul's movements. It has to do with our general attitude to God. If we are on the whole living our faith; avoiding serious sin and honestly confessing all venial sin; living some kind of regular prayer life; and endeavoring to overcome what we know to be our habitual faults — if all this is true, then our soul is most likely in a state of grace, and the inner atmosphere is such that the good angel can come and go as he pleases. We will be on familiar terms with the holy angels, and their communications will be recognizable by their appealing, almost amicable manner.

The influence and inspiration of the good angel will be mild, agreeable and in accord with the status of our disposition. He may at times have to be more severe with us than with others, but he will never have to break into the house like a burglar.

This is the whole point of the third rule. If we observe the overall constitution of our spiritual lives, we can learn to discern the origin of inspiration by seeing how it tallies with that constitution. For if we are living a negligent spiritual life, tolerating serious sin, babying our faults and avoiding the sacraments — in this case, it will be the Evil One who finds our house with doors open and a welcome sign in the front yard. *He* will be our familiar friend in this case. And the good angel will be the one who is only able to get close to us by making some kind of noise or by using some attention-getter. Holy angels, nonetheless, never revert to the base methods of the demons, who have no respect for our free wills.

In the end, they cannot really force us, although this hardly keeps them from trying. The angels, on the other hand, strive to awaken our conscience and not intimidate our will. They want to convince us, not coerce us.

These three practical rules give us some general pointers in discerning the "spirits" that move our souls. Needless to say, the very best help is prayer, purification through repentance and preferably also the counsel of a spiritual director, if you have the good fortune to have one. Today, that is not always possible, but God will not abandon those who do their best with what they have.

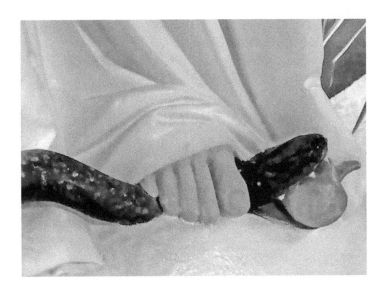

9

The Woman and the Serpent

I N ALL THE ARTWORK OF THE WORLD, THERE is no picture of the Devil which so perfectly conveys the whole predicament of demonic rebellion as does the one we know so well. I am referring to the statue of the delicate Virgin Mary, a mere maiden, with one of her tiny, feminine feet planted almost playfully across the head of an ugly, screeching serpent. The incongruity of Mary's innocent and fragile youth standing almost nonchalantly atop the ghastly head of God's oldest and most powerful enemy at first takes us aback. The sweet wholesomeness of the Virgin's statue, with maybe white billowing clouds above and angelic figures beneath, seems an unlikely setting for a slithering reptile. But there he is, and there he must be.

If we were to ask what Our Lady's relationship to the Devil is, we would have to say bluntly: she has no relationship to the Devil. She never did and never will. She is so far out of his reach, and her thoughts and deeds so many light-years away from his most magnetic incantations, that it is not possible for her to stand in any meaningful rapport with him — that is, except when he's out of sight beneath her foot. Certainly, he fears her, and thus avoids her. As we quoted already from the Apocalypse, he has gone off to wage war on her children instead. To be sure, one form of this warfare will be to attack her children's faith and love. This has conspicuously been the case in our own times. But when she does show up in his proximity, his reaction is one of cowardice.

Now why? This is, after all, a big and powerful devil we are talking about; in fact, in a way he is the "biggest" creature that exists. Why should he be petrified with terror at the mere name of Mary? Some exorcists testify that she is the only person they never hear the devils speaking ill of. Our Lord gets his share of sarcasm and mockery, but somehow, they balk at the idea of taunting Mary. Now something very deep in the whole drama of salvation is at work here. We are at the heartbeat of the whole living system of Marian devotion. We will do well to dwell on this for the rest of this chapter. No better meditation could serve as a conclusion to any book on the world of the angels.

Mary at the Beginning

Holy Scripture begins and ends with Mary. The opening reference is in the third chapter of Genesis:

> And the Lord God said to the serpent: Because you have done this thing, you are cursed among all cattle, and beasts of the earth. Upon your belly you shall go, and earth you shall eat all the days of your life. I will put enmity between you and the Woman, and your seed and her seed: she shall crush your head, and you shall lie in wait for her heel. (Gn. 3:14–15)

The whole Catholic tradition — and with it, scores of painters and sculptors — have seen Our Lady as the one who would crush the head of the Serpent. Biblical scholars may point out that the pronoun of the text (according to some manuscripts) is neuter, thus referring to the seed and not to a woman. The Old Vulgate, the official Bible of the Church for centuries, used the feminine pronoun, as did many of the Fathers in their commentaries. And inspired by these texts, the sculptors of Christendom began configuring plaster or carving stone into serpents and inserting them dutifully below the dainty toes of the Virgin.

We will leave the grammatical squabbles to the experts. They are hardly relevant to the core meaning of the passage. That Our Lady was able to crush the head of Satan did indeed depend entirely upon her Seed, Jesus Christ. It was by her Seed that she crushed it; the Seed crushed it through her. Either formulation could inspire another shipment of statues.

These are the opening chapters of the Old Testament, in the very heart of the story of man's first disobedience. The Holy Spirit has breathed the thought of Mary like a flowered fragrance right over the words that express God's curse. We should take heart in such a breath of life. And Christendom always has.

Christ's humanity was the grand instrument with which God saved the world. But he did not make Jesus from the dust, as he had Adam. He drew his Flesh and Blood from the womb of the Immaculate Virgin. She gave Body and Blood to God, and with it, God saved the nature that bore them. And that Sacred Humanity, the Seed that was one day to come, would be the Redeemer even of her immaculate self. That is to say, Mary's Immaculate Conception was the first fruit of the Seed's redemptive act. Once again, God turns things topsy-turvy, even time itself. But isn't this enough to show that the real crusher of the Serpent's head was this first fruit of the Redemption? And does not this slight grammatical ambiguity actually witness, in its own way, to the incomprehensible fullness of the mystery?

If any part of Scripture needs to be read with the faith of a child, it is this passage. Memorize the words, and repeat them, as exorcists often do to make the impure spirits writhe and finally be off:

> *"She shall crush your head, and you shall lie in wait for her heal."*

Mary at the End

Now take between your fingers the whole bulk of the Bible which lies between Genesis 3 and the Apocalypse, and turn it all like one colossal page so that Scripture falls open to the twelfth chapter of that final book. Moses, David, all the prophets and even our Lord and his Apostles go sailing by as you polish off eons with this one flourish of the hand. Now you are in the final scenario of St. John's cataclysmic vision. Trumpets have just sounded, seven to be exact. But now, with hardly a warning, the whole, galloping pace of the Apocalypse comes to a sudden halt. St. John's eyes open even wider than usual as a new vision spreads across the firmament. After the alarming encounter with Christ in the first chapter, he again sees a face he had known on earth. The evangelist is an old man by now. But he could never forget the face of Mary.

"Then God's temple in heaven was opened, and the ark of his covenant was seen within his temple; and there were flashes of lightning, voices, peals of thunder, an earthquake, and heavy hail. And a great sign appeared in heaven, a Woman clothed with the sun, with the moon under her feet, and on her head a crown of twelve stars" (Apoc. 11:19–12:1).

St. John had stood with Mary under the Cross, and after Our Lord's Ascension cared for her for several years in Ephesus. No Apostle had been closer to the Lord, and no one so close to his Mother. So just as the Apostle had been thrown to the ground with awe when he met Jesus anew in his glory, he was likewise astounded as he gazed upon this most uncommon new perspective on the glories of the Virgin.

Here again, finicky exegetes may try to interrupt our meditation. I would prefer not to allow their worries to cloud our sky right now. That sky is full of lightning and thunder as it is. Let me only remark that in the Apocalypse, as in Genesis, Mary is presented to us in a vast, trans-temporal perspective. We are so accustomed to seeing her in the Gospel, demure and docile in her chamber as St. Gabriel arrives; quietly gazing upon the tiny Christ Child in Bethlehem; humbly and sometimes unsuccessfully endeavoring to get close to her Son during his public life; and finally, standing erect and silent beneath the Cross. These mysteries of Mary, I suppose legitimately, have monopolized our meditations. But ever since Pius IX was inspired to solemnly define her Immaculate Conception in the middle of the 19th century, and Pius XII her Bodily Assumption in the middle of the 20th, that monopoly has been broken.

Mary in Genesis and Mary in the Apocalypse; Mary at the beginning, and Mary at the end—these are overwhelming mysteries that throw a light on Our Lady which makes us reach for titles like Queen of the Universe, Immaculate Conception, Army Set in Battle Array. We will never abandon the titles of Mother and Refuge, but today we need her strength as well as her solace. She was silent in the Gospel. All her words could be printed in a short paragraph — with, however, one conspicuous exception. A day arrived in which she gave full articulate vent to her inner joy, and that was when she, with Child, encountered her cousin, also with child, and intoned the first *Magnificat*.

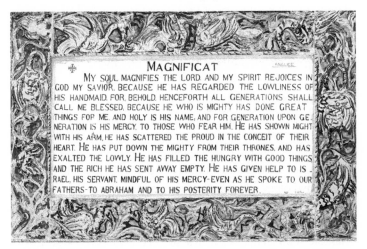

MAGNIFICAT   ANGUKE

MY SOUL MAGNIFIES THE LORD. AND MY SPIRIT REJOICES IN GOD MY SAVIOR, BECAUSE HE HAS REGARDED THE LOWLINESS OF HIS HANDMAID. FOR, BEHOLD, HENCEFORTH ALL GENERATIONS SHALL CALL ME BLESSED, BECAUSE HE WHO IS MIGHTY HAS DONE GREAT THINGS FOR ME, AND HOLY IS HIS NAME, AND FOR GENERATION UPON GENERATION IS HIS MERCY, TO THOSE WHO FEAR HIM. HE HAS SHOWN MIGHT WITH HIS ARM, HE HAS SCATTERED THE PROUD IN THE CONCEIT OF THEIR HEART. HE HAS PUT DOWN THE MIGHTY FROM THEIR THRONES, AND HAS EXALTED THE LOWLY. HE HAS FILLED THE HUNGRY WITH GOOD THINGS. AND THE RICH HE HAS SENT AWAY EMPTY. HE HAS GIVEN HELP TO ISRAEL, HIS SERVANT, MINDFUL OF HIS MERCY-EVEN AS HE SPOKE TO OUR FATHERS-TO ABRAHAM AND TO HIS POSTERITY FOREVER.

The *Magnificat*

The lyrics of Mary's song sound like babble to the ears of the underworld. But Satan's swan song in heaven (probably some version of "My Way") must make perfect sense to them. Our Lady was only truly vocal in the Gospel the one time she sang. And the song she sang, the *Magnificat*, is all about being big (in Latin, *magnus*). But as we know, Mary is singing about the magnitude of God, not of Mary. So unlike the narcissistic monologues of sin. Mary's grandeur is based upon her pure praise of God's magnitude. That is what makes her great. And it is this greatness into which she silently grows in the Gospel, and that turns her ever more into the terror of demons.

When her power is prophetically glimpsed in Genesis, chapter 3, the "great" Satan is already foreseen just below the lowly Maiden.

But when she is gazed upon by St. John in the Book of Revelation, more than her heel is mentioned. She was "clothed with the sun, with the moon under her feet, and on her head a crown of twelve stars": the "sun" of that glorified Sacred Humanity she had given to her Son, the "moon" representing the whole material creation at her feet, and the stars of the angels of heaven about her head like a halo. This is Mary the Magnificent. But she achieved that magnificence by way of humility. God "looked upon the lowliness of his handmaid," and "henceforth all generations will call [her] blessed" (Lk. 1:48). She stands high above the tide of times. But that is not all. The Woman of the Apocalypse also represents her other child, the Church.

Judith once asked God to use her femininity to put an end to the arrogant Holofernes and the Assyrians, and thus "crush their arrogance by the hand of a woman" (Jud. 9:10). Every strapping young man will concede one of his most dreaded nightmares as a boy was to be beaten, even at billiards, by a girl. Well, God has put this psychological principle to good use.

In the Gospel, Satan never got near her. In Genesis, however, it was prophesied that he would snap at her heel. Here, a little Greek mythology will be of service. It is said that the Greek warrior Achilles was dipped as a baby by his mother into a magic river to make him immortal; but his mother held on to his heel while he went under, such that the heel was never washed with invulnerability. One day, an arrow sunk into that heel, and the great warrior was dead.

Mary's heel, however, is another case altogether. Not only is it part of an invulnerable foot of defense, but it is an offensive weapon as well. When God finally unites all things in Christ, and brings Mary's angelic subjects, human children and material adornments into a beautiful array around her Immaculate Conception, that little foot of hers will step forth. It will be as if she had just caught sight of a tiny bug; and without anyone giving notice, the high conceits of hell will have been flattened forever. The Serpent's snapping mouth and arrogant face will have lifted themselves for the last time. The Achilles' heel of Satan is his head.

CONCLUSION

S T. AUGUSTINE SAID WE SHOULD REGARD
the Devil as a vicious dog on a chain. He can bark wildly and
at times be impossible to ignore, but he can only bite us if
we stray into the radius of his chain. In a related image, St. Francis
de Sales says the Devil continues baying at the door of our souls,
precisely because we have *not* let him in. Thus, whether it is you
who enter the circle of the chained dog, so that his biting keeps
him from barking, or the Devil who enters your soul by invitation,
so that he has no reason for barking—in both cases, you were
better off with the barks. For as we say, barking dogs don't bite.

They do, however, keep us on our toes. We began our consideration of fallen angels by remarking upon the danger and excitement
of Christian warfare. Besides this, I hope we have gained some
understanding into why God permits the malice of the Devil to
begin with. We should better understand now how it finally stands
in the service of higher goods God is already preparing, invisible
to our eyes but always accessible to our hope.

Even so, the "mystery of iniquity" (1 Thess. 2:7) will never be
fully grasped, just as darkness can never become visible. What
we *can* do is appreciate how wonderful the brightness of truth
is and how it is cast into an unmistakable profile by the gloom
and shadows that try to overcome it. All they do is make it more
conspicuous, as the frame does for a painting or the setting does
for a jewel. And in this way, we learn better to endure times of
darkness precisely because we have already glimpsed the light—the
Divine Light—at the proverbial end of the tunnel.

The New Testament teaches us that "for those who love God,
all things work together unto good" (Rom. 8:28). Even the things
the Devil does work together for someone's good, though hardly
for his own. And yet there is a sense we can just barely grasp in
which it is good for evil to have had its hour. Even the demons
have a place in the plot, for in the end, each of us—holy and
unholy—will have "to go to *his own* place" (Acts 1:25). In heaven,

we will not be bothered at all by the "problem of evil." What seems to be an enigma here on earth will no longer concern anyone at all.

Still, there is one last and definitive comment to make about the fallen spirits. And I think there is no better way to conclude our meditation than by highlighting it. It also serves as a final image to take with us at the end of our book about the angels. It is perhaps the best answer ever given to the mystery of iniquity, and it may very well surprise our readers.

It is said that the medieval mystic Julian of Norwich (early 15th century) was permitted by God to have a vision of the fall of the Devil at the beginning of time. The mystic is reported to have broken out into such infectious laughter that all who were in the room started laughing along with her. Speaking of how Christ stood his ground in the face of the Devil, she declares: "I saw Christ scorn the malice of the Adversary and thoroughly dismiss him as powerless, and I saw that he wants us to discount him, too. This made me laugh out loud, which made the people around me laugh. Their laughter brought me great delight."[1]

At the end of this long reflection on fallen angels, and indeed of our entire book on the angels, our conclusion must be the following: there is quite simply no symmetry at all between the goodness of the angels and the evil of the demons. Darkness cannot live without the light, but when history is over, the light will get on just fine without the dark. The dark is, in the fullest sense of the term, *lost* without the light.

Theologians tell us that evil is a privation of the good, a kind of absence. To be sure, the beings in which such a privation exist are very real, the experience of such a lack is very real, and the consequences of the absence are quite real. But at the heart of evil lies a vacuum, a pure and hollow negation, and one that will ultimately be swallowed up into the nothingness it prefers.

Goodness is powerful, bright and alive — creative, imaginative and surprising — unendingly renewable and incurably hopeful. Evil is just dark and ultimately vacuous. Furthermore, we find loads of

---

1   Mirabai Starr, *Showings of Julian of Norwich: A New Translation* (Newburyport, MA: Hampton Roads: 2013), chap. 13, p. 1.

good cheer and healthy humor in goodness, but evil has to twist itself into pretzels just to generate a snicker.

So, what on earth was Julian of Norwich laughing about? Perhaps she fully realized that yes, the Devil is malicious, a perfectly horrible creature, a murderer, a liar, an accuser, our sworn enemy and our daily tempter. But if there was one thing she saw in him that must have summed up his infernal antics with consummate accuracy, it was this: the Devil is ridiculous.

APPENDIX

PRAYERS OF EXORCISM FOR THE LAITY

St. Michael's Prayer (short form):
St. Michael the Archangel, defend us in battle.
Be our protection against the wickedness and snares of the Devil;
May God rebuke him, we humbly pray,
And do thou, O Prince of the heavenly hosts, by the power of God,
Thrust into hell Satan, and all the evil spirits who prowl about the
  world seeking the ruin of souls. Amen.

St. Michael's Prayer (long form):
O glorious Prince of the heavenly host, St. Michael the Archangel, defend us in the battle and in the fearful warfare that we are
waging against the principalities and powers, against the rulers of
this world of darkness, against the evil spirits. Come to the assistance of men, whom Almighty God created immortal, making them
in his own image and likeness and redeeming them at a great price
from the tyranny of Satan. Fight this day the battle of the Lord
with your legions of holy angels, even as of old you fought against
Lucifer, the leader of the proud spirits and all his rebel angels, who
were powerless to stand against you, neither was their place found
any more in heaven. And that apostate angel, transformed into an
angel of darkness who still creeps about the earth to encompass our
ruin, was cast headlong into the abyss together with his followers.
But behold, that first enemy of mankind, and a murderer from the
beginning, has regained his confidence. Changing himself into an
angel of light, he goes about with the whole multitude of the wicked
spirits to invade the earth and blot out the Name of God and of
his Christ, to plunder, to slay and to consign to eternal damnation
the souls that have been destined for a crown of everlasting life.
This wicked serpent, like an unclean torrent, pours into men of
depraved minds and corrupt hearts the poison of his malice, the
spirit of lying, impiety and blasphemy, and the deadly breath of
impurity and every form of vice and iniquity. These crafty enemies
of mankind have filled to overflowing with gall and wormwood the
Church, which is the Bride of the Lamb without spot; they have
laid profane hands upon her most sacred treasures. Make haste,

therefore, O invincible Prince, to help the people of God against the inroads of the lost spirits and grant us the victory. Amen. (Leo XIII's *Motu Proprio*, Sept. 25, 1888)

[N O T E : Pope Leo's "Exorcism of Satan and the Fallen Angels," issued also in 1888, was intended only for bishops and authorized priests.]

Prayer of the Cross
Ecce signum Crucis, recedite inimici lucis!
In Nomine Patris et Filii et Spiritus Sancti. Amen.
Behold the Sign of the Cross, Begone all enemies of light!
In the Name of the Father, and of the Son, and of the Holy Spirit. Amen.

General Deprecatory Exorcism
Lord, let us be placed under the exorcistic power of the Name of Jesus, the Blood of Jesus, and the Face of Jesus, that no attack of the Enemy can do us harm. In the Name of the Father, and of the Son, and of the Holy Spirit. Amen.

ON THE USE OF THE SACRAMENTALS

Holy water

A properly designated bottle can be kept in the home and filled at your church's supply (or blessed by a priest using the *Ritual*'s formula of blessing, if your parish has no supply). One may keep a stoup of one's own always filled, perhaps near the front door (out of reach of children and pets!), so that one can bless oneself on entering and exiting. We need not overdo it. But we can use this sacramental in the spirit of freedom of a child of God, trusting in his help, and knowing that finally, the greater good will prevail. As with all sacramentals, it ought to be used with moderation and dignity.

Blessed objects

We gain further powerful protection against malefic influences by making pious use of other specially blessed objects. They may also be kept in the home, such as a properly blessed Crucifix, hanging conspicuously on the wall of the family room. Smaller crucifixes may even be hung in other important rooms, including bedrooms. But again, dignity and measure ought to be observed. There is a broad selection of possibilities, something to everyone's taste and temperament. These images, like the others, can also be blessed by a priest according to the Church's *Ritual*.

Items worn on the body

One is, of course, not always at home, nor in a church, and yet some of the greatest dangers may be met at these times. The Church has recommended and enriched with indulgences a variety of scapulars and medals. Any one of the several kinds of scapular is a kind of substitute for a religious habit. Such habits are subjected to special blessings for those who will wear them in religious life. The pious wearing of a scapular is the next best thing. The various medals, however, and especially the Miraculous Medal, offer a comparable share in heaven's special protection. One medal, the St. Benedict's Medal, is of such exceptional power that we shall treat of it under a separate heading.

Relics

A special mention must be given to the keeping and veneration of the relics of the saints, and of objects which in some way came in contact with Our Lord, Our Lady and the places and events around them, or with one of the saints. Although some wish to mock the veneration and use of such relics, usually in the same breath with an appeal to return to the early Church, it seems they have not read very far into the Acts of the Apostles. In chapter 19, we read that "handkerchiefs or aprons were carried away from his [St. Paul's] body to the sick, and diseases left them and the evil spirits came out of them."

THE SAINT BENEDICT MEDAL

THIS OLD AND POWERFUL SACRAMENTAL
deserves an in-depth treatment, as it gives a kind of practical incarnation of the main purpose of the second part of this book. This medal has long been regarded as especially efficacious in protecting its wearers against demonic attacks and securing a number of special graces. Let us take a closer look at the inscriptions on its two sides.

On the front of the medal we find St. Benedict holding a Cross in one hand and the Rule of St. Benedict in the other. At his sides are the words "*Crux S. Patris Benedicti*" ("The Cross of the Holy Father Benedict"), and below his feet: "*Ex S M Casino MDCCCLXXX*" ("From the holy Mount of Casino, 1880"). On that date, Monte Casino was given the exclusive right to produce this medal, and special Jubilee indulgences were added. Still on this front side of the medal we find inscribed in a circle the words: "*Ejus in obitu nostro presentia muniamur*" ("May his presence protect us in our hour of death").

The reverse side of the medal is where the real exorcistic force reveals itself. In the center is a Cross. The Cross, which St. Benedict so loved and often used as a powerful exorcism, is the sign before which even Dracula flinched. The vertical beam of the Cross bears the letters C. S. S. M. L., and the horizontal beam the letters N. D. S. M. D. These are the first letters of the words:

CRUX SACRA SIT MIHI LUX
May the Holy Cross be a light unto me,

NON DRACO SIT MIHI DUX
And may the Dragon never be my guide.

The four large letters at the corners of the Cross, C S P B, stand for:

CRUX SANCTI PATRIS BENEDICTI
The Cross of the Holy Father Benedict

We are not through yet. In addition to the *Pax* (peace) motto at the top, we find the following letters in a circle around the margin of this side: V. R. S. N. S. M. V., S. M. Q. L. I. V. B. It almost looks Masonic; except, of course, the Benedictines are quite willing to tell you what the letters stand for, and they are enough to make any secret society get the shakes:

VADE RETRO SATANA
Get behind me, Satan;

NUNQUAM SUADE MIHI VANA.
Never suggest vain thoughts to me.

SUNT MALA QUAE LIBAS;
The cup you offer is evil;

IPSE VENENA BIBAS!
Drink the poison yourself!

This richly indulgenced medal can be worn around the neck, be attached to one's Rosary or simply kept in a pocket or purse. The pious intention of wearing such an object, together with the Church's powerful blessing and intercessory power, make it into an unspoken prayer which has been shown to be of great help in maintaining holy purity, bringing about conversions, and protecting against inclement weather and contagious disease.

SUGGESTED FURTHER READING

Andrejev, Vladislav. *The Angel of the Countenance of God: Theology and Iconology of Theophanies.* Translated by Alex Apatov. New York: Angelico Press, 2021.

Bonino, Serge-Thomas. *Angels and Demons: A Catholic Introduction.* Translated by Michael Miller. Washington, D.C: Catholic University of America Press, 2016.

Collins, James. *The Thomistic Philosophy of the Angels.* Washington D.C: Catholic University of America Press, 1947.

Daniélou, Jean. *The Angels and Their Mission.* Translated by David Heiman. Allen, Texas: Thomas More Publishing, 1987.

Davidson, Gustav. *A Dictionary of Angels — Including the Fallen Angels.* New York: Free Press, 1994.

Heiser, Michael S. *The Unseen Realm: Recovering the Supernatural Worldview of the Bible.* Kindle version. Bellingham, WA: Lexham Press, 2015.

Hoffmann, Tobias, ed. *A Companion to Angels in Medieval Philosophy.* Leiden-Boston: Brill, 2012.

Horgan, John. *His Angels at Our Side.* Irondale, AL: EWTN Publishing, 2018.

Keck, David. *Angels & Angelology in the Middle Ages.* Oxford: Oxford University Press, 1998.

Muehlberger, Ellen. *Angels in Late Ancient Christianity.* Oxford: Oxford University Press, 2015.

Parente, Pascal. *The Angels: In Catholic Teaching and Tradition.* Charlotte, NC: TAN Books, 2013.

Peterson, Eric. *The Angels and the Liturgy.* Translated by Ronald Walls. New York: Herder & Herder, 1964.

SOME RECENT CHURCH DOCUMENTS
REGARDING ANGELS

CATECHISM OF THE CATHOLIC CHURCH, 1992
from Part I: Section 2, Chapter 1, Article 1, Paragraph 5, I

HEAVEN AND EARTH

325 The Apostles' Creed professes that God is "creator of heaven and earth." The Nicene Creed makes it explicit that this profession includes "all that is, seen and unseen."

326 The Scriptural expression "heaven and earth" means all that exists, creation in its entirety. It also indicates the bond, deep within creation, that both unites heaven and earth and distinguishes the one from the other: "the earth" is the world of men, while "heaven" or "the heavens" can designate both the firmament and God's own "place"—"our Father in heaven" and consequently the "heaven" too which is eschatological glory. Finally, "heaven" refers to the saints and the "place" of the spiritual creatures, the angels, who surround God.[186]

327 The profession of faith of the Fourth Lateran Council (1215) affirms that God "from the beginning of time made at once (*simul*) out of nothing both orders of creatures, the spiritual and the corporeal, that is, the angelic and the earthly, and then (*deinde*) the human creature, who as it were shares in both orders, being composed of spirit and body."[187]

I. THE ANGELS
The existence of angels—a truth of faith

328 The existence of the spiritual, non-corporeal beings that Sacred Scripture usually calls "angels" is a truth of faith. The witness of Scripture is as clear as the unanimity of Tradition.

Who are they?

329 St. Augustine says: "'Angel' is the name of their office, not of their nature. If you seek the name of their nature, it is 'spirit'; if you seek the name of their office, it is 'angel': from what they are, 'spirit', from what they do, 'angel.'"[188] With their whole beings the angels are servants and messengers of God. Because they "always behold the face of my Father who is in heaven" they are the "mighty ones who do his word, hearkening to the voice of his word."[189]

330 As purely spiritual creatures angels have intelligence and will: they are personal and immortal creatures, surpassing in perfection all visible creatures, as the splendor of their glory bears witness.[190]

Christ "with all his angels"

331 Christ is the center of the angelic world. They are his angels: "When the Son of man comes in his glory, and all the angels with him . . . ."[191] They belong to him because they were created through and for him: "for in him all things were created in heaven and on earth, visible and invisible, whether thrones or dominions or principalities or authorities—all things were created through him and for him."[192] They belong to him still more because he has made them messengers of his saving plan: "Are they not all ministering spirits sent forth to serve, for the sake of those who are to obtain salvation?"[193]

332 Angels have been present since creation and throughout the history of salvation, announcing this salvation from afar or near and serving the accomplishment of the divine plan: they closed the earthly paradise; protected Lot; saved Hagar and her child; stayed Abraham's hand; communicated the law by their ministry; led the People of God; announced births and callings; and assisted the prophets, just to cite a few examples.[194] Finally, the angel Gabriel announced the birth of the Precursor and that of Jesus himself.[195]

333 From the Incarnation to the Ascension, the life of the Word incarnate is surrounded by the adoration and service of angels. When God "brings the firstborn into the world, he says: 'Let all God's angels worship him.'"[196] Their song of praise at the birth of Christ has not ceased resounding in the Church's praise: "Glory to God in the highest!"[197] They protect Jesus in his infancy, serve him in the desert, strengthen him in his agony in the garden, when he could have been saved by them from the hands of his enemies as Israel had been.[198] Again, it is the angels who "evangelize" by proclaiming the Good News of Christ's Incarnation and Resurrection.[199] They will be present at Christ's return, which they will announce, to serve at his judgement.[200]

The angels in the life of the Church

334 In the meantime, the whole life of the Church benefits from the mysterious and powerful help of angels.[201]

335 In her liturgy, the Church joins with the angels to adore the thrice-holy God. She invokes their assistance (in the Roman Canon's *Supplices te rogamus* . . . ["Almighty God, we pray that your angel . . ."]; in the funeral liturgy's *In Paradisum deducant te angeli* . . . ["May the angels lead you into Paradise . . ."]). Moreover, in the "Cherubic Hymn" of the Byzantine Liturgy, she celebrates the memory of certain angels more particularly (St. Michael, St. Gabriel, St. Raphael, and the guardian angels).

336 From infancy to death human life is surrounded by their watchful care and intercession.[202] "Beside each believer stands an angel as protector and shepherd leading him to life."[203] Already here on earth the Christian life shares by faith in the blessed company of angels and men united in God.

IN BRIEF

350 *Angels are spiritual creatures who glorify God without ceasing and who serve his saving plans for other creatures: "The angels work together for the benefit of us all" (St. Thomas Aquinas, STh I, 114, 3, ad 3).*

351 *The angels surround Christ their Lord. They serve him especially in the accomplishment of his saving mission to men.*

352 *The Church venerates the angels who help her on her earthly pilgrimage and protect every human being.*

353 *God willed the diversity of his creatures and their own particular goodness, their interdependence and their order. He destined all material creatures for the good of the human race. Man, and through him all creation, is destined for the glory of God.*

354 *Respect for laws inscribed in creation and the relations which derive from the nature of things is a principle of wisdom and a foundation for morality.*

186 Pss 115:16; 19:2; Mt 5:16.
187 Lateran Council IV (1215): DS 800; cf. DS 3002 and Paul VI, CPG #8.
188 St. Augustine, *En. in Ps.* 103, 1, 15: PL 37, 1348.
189 Mt 18:10; Ps 103:20.
190 Cf. Pius XII, *Humani generis:* DS 3891; Lk 20:36; Dan 10:9–12.
191 Mt 25:31.
192 Col 1:16.
193 Heb 1:14.
194 Cf. Job 38:7 (where angels are called "sons of God"); Gen 3:24; 19; 21:17; 22:11; Acts 7:53; Ex 23:20–23; Judg 13; 6:11–24; Is 6:6; 1 Kings 19:5.
195 Cf. Lk 1:11, 26.
196 Heb 1:6.
197 Lk 2:14.
198 Cf. Mt 1:20; 2:13,19; 4:11; 26:53; Mk 1:13; Lk 22:43; 2 Macc 10:29–30; 11:8.
199 Cf. Lk 2:8–14; Mk 16:5–7.
200 Cf. Acts 1:10–11; Mt 13:41; 24:31; Lk 12:8–9.
201 Cf. Acts 5:18–20; 8:26–29; 10:3–8; 12:6–11; 27:23–25.
202 Cf. Mt 18:10; Lk 16:22; Pss 34:7; 91:10–13; Job 33:23–24; Zech 1:12; Tob 12:12.
203 St. Basil, *Adv. Eunomium* III, I: PG 29, 656B.
204 Gen 1:1–2:4.

CATECHISM OF THE CATHOLIC CHURCH, 1992
from Part I: Section 2, Chapter I, Article I, Paragraph 7, 2

II. THE FALL OF THE ANGELS

391 Behind the disobedient choice of our first parents lurks a seductive voice, opposed to God, which makes them fall into death out of envy.[266] Scripture and the Church's Tradition see in this being a fallen angel, called "Satan" or the "devil."[267] The Church teaches that Satan was at first a good angel, made by God: "The devil and the other demons were indeed created naturally good by God, but they became evil by their own doing."[268]

392 Scripture speaks of a sin of these angels.[269] This "fall" con-sists in the free choice of these created spirits, who radically and irrevocably rejected God and his reign. We find a reflection of that rebellion in the tempter's words to our first parents: "You will be like God."[270] The devil "has sinned from the beginning"; he is "a liar and the father of lies."[271]

393 It is the irrevocable character of their choice, and not a defect in the infinite divine mercy, that makes the angels' sin unforgivable. "There is no repentance for the angels after their fall, just as there is no repentance for men after death."[272]

394 Scripture witnesses to the disastrous influence of the one Jesus calls "a murderer from the beginning," who would even try to divert Jesus from the mission received from his Father.[273] "The reason the Son of God appeared was to destroy the works of the devil."[274] In its consequences the gravest of these works was the mendacious seduction that led man to disobey God.

395 The power of Satan is, nonetheless, not infinite. He is only a creature, powerful from the fact that he is pure spirit, but still a creature. He cannot prevent the building up of God's reign. Although Satan may act in the world out of hatred for God and his kingdom in Christ Jesus, and although his action may cause grave injuries — of a spiritual nature and, indirectly, even of a physical nature — to each man and to society, the action is permitted by divine providence which with strength and gentleness guides human and cosmic history. It is a great mystery that providence should permit diabolical activity, but "we know that in everything God works for good with those who love him."[275]

267 Cf Jn 8:44; Rev 12:9.
268 Lateran Council IV (1215): DS 800.
269 Cf. 2 Pt 2:4.
270 Gen 3:5.
271 1 Jn 3:8; Jn 8:44.
272 St. John Damascene, *De fide orth.* 2, 4: PG 94, 877.
273 Jn 8:44; cf. Mt 4:1–11.
274 1 Jn 3:8.
275 Rom 8:28.

(All *Catechism texts taken from* https://www.vatican.va/archive/ENG0015/_INDEX.HTM)

OTHER DOCUMENTS

In 591, Pope St. Gregory the Great delivered a famous homily (nr. 34), commenting on Luke 15, 1–20 and Christ's remark about the joy among the angels of heaven over one sinner who repents. Within the homily the pope speaks at length about the nine choirs of angels, their attributes and tasks. A translation of the homily can be read here: https://sites.google.com/site/aquinasstudybible/home/luke-commentary/gregory-the-great-homily-34-on-the-gospels.

"Christian Faith and Demonology," printed from *L'Osservatore Romano*, English edition, July 10, 1975, in pamphlet form by the Daughters of St. Paul. This study was commissioned by the Congregation for the Doctrine of the Faith and gives a thorough overview of the Church's teaching on demonology: http://www.vatican.va/roman_curia/congregations/cfaith/documents/rc_con_cfaith_doc_19750626_fede-cristiana-demonologia_en.html.

From the Catechism of the Catholic Church, "On the Fall": https://www.vatican.va/archive/ccc_css/archive/catechism/p1s2c1p7.htm.

"...That Evil Which is Called the Devil," Pope Paul VI. This pamphlet contains the text of the Holy Father's 1972 address on the fallen angels, printed also by the Daughters of St. Paul. Available online at https://www.ewtn.com/catholicism/library/confronting-the-devils-power-8986.

Vatican II references to demons can be found in Austin Flannery, ed., *Documents of Vatican II* (Eerdmans, 1975), pp. 4, 352, 368, 392, 823, 914, 915, 936.

The text of the 1987 address on spiritual warfare, delivered by Pope John Paul II at the sanctuary of St. Michael in Monte Gargano, Italy, is available in the journal *The Voice of Padre Pio*, vol. XVII, No. 11, 1987, pp. 22–23.

Pope John Paul II's 1986 catechesis on the angels, especially the audiences of August 13 and 20, are printed in *Oh Angel of God My Guardian Dear*, by National Center for Padre Pio, Inc.

Pope Francis on the Devil: https://catholicherald.co.uk/news/2019/05/01/satan-is-real-pope-francis-says/.

ABOUT THE AUTHOR

FR. SCOTT RANDALL PAINE is a priest of the archdiocese of Brasilia, Brazil, and professor of medieval philosophy and Eastern thought at the city's federal university. A convert to the Catholic faith in 1973, he was ordained by Pope St. John Paul II in 1983, took his doctorate in philosophy in Rome and has since lived, studied, and taught in Europe, Asia, and South America. His collection of essays by Bernard Kelly, *A Catholic Mind Awake*, and the second edition of his study of G. K. Chesterton, *The Universe and Mr. Chesterton*, were both published by Angelico Press. Paine's current writing can be followed on the website: 3wisdoms.com.